The Open Adoption Book

THE OPEN ADOPTION BOOK

A Guide to Adoption without Tears

BRUCE M. RAPPAPORT, PH.D.

Macmillan Publishing Company
NEW YORK

Maxwell Macmillan Canada
TORONTO

Maxwell Macmillan International
NEW YORK   OXFORD   SINGAPORE   SYDNEY

Macmillan Publishing Company   Maxwell Macmillan Canada, Inc.
866 Third Avenue   1200 Eglinton Avenue East
New York, NY 10022   Suite 200
                                      Don Mills, Ontario M3C 3N1

Macmillan Publishing Company is part of the Maxwell Communication Group of Companies.

Library of Congress Cataloging-in-Publication Data
Rappaport, Bruce M.
    The open adoption book : a guide to adoption without tears / Bruce M. Rappaport.
        p. cm.
    Includes index.
    ISBN 0-02-601105-0
    1. Open adoption—United States. I. Title.
HV875.55.R37 1992
362.7'34'0973—dc20   91-42800   CIP

Macmillan books are available at special discounts for bulk purchases for sales promotions, premiums, fund-raising, or educational use. For details, contact:

Special Sales Director
Macmillan Publishing Company
866 Third Avenue
New York, NY 10022

10 9 8 7 6 5 4 3 2 1

Printed in the United States of America

To Anna,
who has made possible the greatest joy in my life:
being her Daddy.

Contents

Acknowledgments

This book is the result of being able to share in the joy of thousands of adopting parents, birthparents, and adopted children. What extraordinary people! And my work at the Independent Adoption Center would simply not have been possible without my partnership with Kathleen Silber, the associate executive director of the Independent Adoption Center and one of the founders of the open adoption movement.

My thanks also to all the people who have stuck with me during the two years of writing this book: especially the wonderful staff of the center and its devoted board of directors. And to the professionals in the writing field who kept me going: Elizabeth Mehren, Carol Mann, and Natalie Chapman.

The Open Adoption Book

Introduction: The Promise
of Open Adoption

*F*or almost a decade, fifteen to twenty people have come
to the Independent Adoption Center each Saturday morning for an informal information session on open adoption.
These women and men are among the staggering one in five
people of childbearing age who face infertility problems. Almost all are married couples—married for anywhere from
six months to twenty years—but some are single women or
men. The age range is typically late twenties to late forties.
They come from large cities and small towns and their jobs
vary from professional to semiskilled to homemaker. They all
share a profound sense that their lives will simply not be
complete until they become parents, or, in some cases, the
parents of another child.

Most of those attending the program have heard that there
is little hope of adopting a healthy child. With infertility sky-

rocketing and the number of babies available for adoption plummeting, adoption appears an almost impossible goal. There are rumors, though, that something called open adoption can change that. But open adoption sounds experimental, complicated, and intimidating. Most people have heard stories, from friends, TV, or the newspapers, of awful tragedies with these new kinds of adoption. They are annoyed and anxious about having to be in some kind of relationship with people called birthmothers or birthfathers. As the program begins, most people wonder if they should just stick to the older, more conventional adoption agencies, even if their odds of succeeding will be lower.

During those mornings at the center, people hear about the problems with closed adoption that gave birth to the new forms of open adoption. We address, in detail, their questions and concerns about open adoption. They learn about the extensive counseling support system that will be available to them and the birthparents. Adopting parents and birthparents who have personally experienced open adoption candidly share their experiences. Somehow, in the course of those three hours, things start to look different. Open adoption seems almost normal, almost feasible. At some moments, the whole process even seems beautiful and touching. They are not fully persuaded, by any means, but they start feeling that this just might be worth a try.

Over a thousand of these couples (and dozens of single people) have overcome their fears and found the extraordinary joy of finding a new baby relatively quickly through an open adoption. Today, they have a hard time remembering why they ever doubted that this was the right way for them to go. But their initial misgivings did not simply disappear. These men and women chose open adoption because someone addressed their deepest fears and responded to their greatest concerns. And that is what I propose to do in this book.

But what is open adoption and why is the process more successful than more traditional, closed approaches? In the older forms of adoption, almost all decisions were made by the professional counselors; neither the adoptive parents nor the birthparents had any real power. All information about all the parties was kept secret, and contact before, during, and after the adoption was not permitted. Open adoption developed out of a rejection of this approach, but as more and more open adoption programs have emerged across the country, defining the exact meaning of the term has become more difficult. Some programs offer only a limited version of open adoption (sometimes called semi-open adoption), while others are characterized by fully open procedures. In brief, in fully open adoption, the birthparents and adopting parents select each other. Rather than outsiders such as social workers, doctors, or lawyers controlling the process, the adopting parents and the biological parents are the ones who have power over the critical decisions in their adoption. They meet in person and share full identifying information with each other. They have the option of ongoing contact over the years, either in person or through correspondence. The type and frequency of this contact is based on the mutual needs of the birthparents, adopting parents, and the adopted child, but some kind of ongoing relationship is the norm. In semi-open adoption, various restrictions are placed on the adoptive parents and birthparents. For instance, the birthparents may only be able to choose from among a limited number of adoptive parents selected by the adoption agency from their list of eligible couples. The exchange of information may also be restricted to first names, and postbirth contact may be limited to indirect communication through the agency.

In sharp contrast to traditional adoption, these open approaches offer genuinely respectful and empowering programs that have a much stronger appeal for young women facing untimely pregnancies. So much so, that if couples do pursue open rather than closed adoption, the odds of their adopting a child within a reasonable amount of time rise dramatically. While there may be sixty infertile couples for every infant available for adoption, a smaller number of prospective adopting couples consider an open adoption. Since most birthparents prefer openness, those adopting parents willing to follow this path can usually adopt a baby within six to eighteen months (or less). What a contrast to the three-, five-, or ten-year waits common through older adoption routes.

Is *The Open Adoption Book* a detailed, step-by-step guide to open adoption? In this book, you will become familiar with the basic procedures of open adoption, but the major focus is broader. Over the years, I have found that the primary obstacles to successful adoptions are not technical but emotional. Most prospective adopting parents are bright and resourceful. With the right type of help and support, they have little trouble meeting the logistical requirements to succeed at an open adoption. *The principal problem is that open adoption can seem so frightening and intimidating that people are reluctant to commit themselves fully enough to the process to make it work for them.*

To start with, the experience of couples with infertility often has been so depressing that they feel trapped on a virtual medical treadmill. They cannot bring themselves to call the treatments to a halt and start pursuing any kind of adoption. If they do decide, finally, to move on to adoption, they may be so demoralized that they choose the most conservative, closed approach, even if it is far less promising. They worry that the birthparents are all desperate women, untrustworthy people who got themselves pregnant inadvertently and should have known better. Will they ever feel like true parents, they wonder, if the adoption is open and the birthparents are so involved? Because of their anguish, many women and men who in other situations would pride themselves on being forward-looking and willing to take reasonable risks are willing to pursue only the most traditional, closed approaches to adoption. Others do pursue open adoption but they do so halfheartedly. Their bouts with infertility have left them isolated and alone and they bring these same emotions to the adoption process. They pursue their adoption without support from friends and family. They shy away from getting counseling though open adoption, by its very nature, requires such support. In the end, many make only the most perfunctory efforts at adoption and soon give up altogether.

This book addresses those deeply felt and legitimate fears. We start with an explanation of why adoption has become so difficult and how open adoption has emerged in response. Against this background, we can turn to the first challenge faced by prospective adopting parents: moving beyond purely medical attempts to solve their infertility toward pursuing adoption as a way to bring a new child into their lives. Then we can go to the heart of the matter. Open adoption is primarily about relationships. There is the relationship between the adopting parents and birthparents before the adoption and their ongoing ties afterward. There is the connection between the birthparents and adopted child. Finally, there are the relationships central to the adoptive family: the ties between the adoptive parents and their adopted child throughout their lifetimes. Most people's greatest fears are about these relationships. Yet, most find that these connections and ties not only work out but become a source of support, stability, and joy for everyone.

Because I am so enthusiastic about open adoption, people often ask me if I believe there are no risks in this process. The answer is that there certainly are risks, especially since adoption has such a profound impact on people's lives. Throughout this book, I will be discussing the hazards involved in open adoption and offering ways to avoid them. But I think some things need to be said about these risks. Often, it is helpful to see these problems in the context of the uncertainties that are almost always part of any *normal* pregnancy, labor, and delivery. Twenty percent of pregnancies end in miscarriage, and perhaps another 20 percent of couples—especially couples in their thirties and forties—face some type of serious risk of problems related to the birth itself. These include possible birth defects, high-risk pregnancies, and difficult deliveries. Moreover, while adoption can be a formidable way to create a family, today a large number of people face an equally difficult challenge: creating a new family after a divorce. At least with adoption, the child is part of the family from birth. In postdivorce situations, the children, having had one set of parents for years, suddenly find themselves with a new set or sets of adults they are expected to relate to as their mother or father. And then there are the myriad disputes over child custody and visitation rights.

The risks of open adoption, though real, are often exaggerated. Because this process is relatively new, open adoption has been the focus of considerable media attention—and the media focus more on problems than on successes. Most media people consider good news boring; what sells is more heart-wrenching stories of loss and tragedy. Word-of-mouth information tends to move in the same direction. For instance, people rarely discuss medical operations that went well; they talk of the disasters. So it is with adoption. And there is another factor that reinforces this tendency to emphasize the negative. Those familiar with the hardships faced by people who have experienced infertility know only too well how weak and vulnerable it can leave men and women feeling. Because of this, when those same people consider adoption, the uncertainties often seem to loom much larger than any of the positive aspects of the process. The risks of open adoption also need to be compared to the very real problems with the other option, closed adoption—a topic I will discuss at length in chapter two. Finally, we need to consider the risk of the ultimate alternative to open adoption: not having children at all. Though there certainly are people whose lives can be and are fulfilled without becoming parents, for many others, such a life would be tragic.

In this book, the problems and difficulties of open adoption will not be ignored, yet the focus will be on the positive side of open adoption. In choosing this as the focus of the book, I realize that I take a risk as an author. I open myself up to accusations of being a Pollyanna or a propagandist. But I am consciously making that choice in this book—as in my professional work—because I have consistently found that it is the positive side of open adoption that is far less known and understood.

The Open Adoption Book is based on my work as the executive director of both the Independent Adoption Center, a nonprofit adoption program primarily based on the West Coast, and the National Federation for Open Adoption Education. The Independent Adoption Center was founded in 1982. At the time, I was the administrative director of an infertility clinic in the San Francisco Bay Area. When the medical staff advised a couple that further medical treatment made little sense, they would turn to me for advice on what to do next. But we had nothing to tell them. We knew if they pursued conventional adoption, the wait would be intolerable. After all, they had already waited years to become parents and typically had gone through two to five years of infertility treatment. We knew there were some attorneys and doctors who seemed to find babies for adoption fairly quickly. Yet we were concerned about the lack of counseling and support in adoption situations which involved such delicate and intense human emotions. A group of us decided to leave the clinic and establish a nonprofit organization committed to humanizing, opening up, and revitalizing the adoption process. We also wanted a program whose main emphasis was on counseling and support before and during the adoption process and throughout the lives of our adoptive families. In the first years of the center, we facilitated perhaps one adoption every six or eight weeks. That was a major accomplishment by conventional adoption agency standards. Today, the center is the largest program of its kind in the United States and facilitates as many as four to eight adoptions every week.

This book is aimed primarily at those who face some type of barrier to having a first or additional child biologically. The information here also may be helpful to those who want to support members of their family, friends, or clients who are experiencing the pain of infertility and considering adoption as a path to parenthood. Throughout this book are comments, anecdotes, and stories from birthparents, birthfathers, birthgrandparents, and adopting parents and their families. Each of these people has participated in a fully open adoption through either a private adoption or an agency adoption, either at the Independent Adoption Center or at one of the other open adoption programs located across the country. In each case, the adopting parents and birthparents located across the country. In each case, the adopting parents and birthparents are well known to each other. Yet people also want their privacy respected so, with a few exceptions, individual names are withheld.

For me, there is simply no greater joy than being a parent. After seven long years of infertility I finally became a father, and the joy has been beyond my wildest expectations. I can still recall the first time that my beautiful daughter, Anna, called me Daddy. I remember wondering then if all my past life had not simply been a matter of passing time waiting for that moment finally to happen to me. My daughter is now thirteen years old and has probably called me Daddy a thousand times or more. Yet sometimes I think I can remember every time she has done so. Through open adoption, this once seemingly impossible dream can now be a reality.

Typical Steps in an Open Adoption

Specific protocols and procedures for open adoption vary from state to state and program to program but these are the typical stages of the process.

1. The age of prospective adopting parents varies from mid-twenties to late fifties, with late thirties to early forties being the most common. Most have been married for five to ten years though newly-weds and single parents also adopt. Most have been through three to five years of fairly extensive infertility treatment. Their first step is an introductory-educational session covering adoption in general and open adoption in particular. This is followed by a home study to evaluate their "readiness" for adoption. In an agency adoption, this is done by the program's social workers; in attorney adoptions, the state itself does the investigation. In the past, many agencies have imposed arbitrary restrictions (such as previous adoptions, age, religion, etc.) about who they would allow to adopt. Today, open adoption agencies approach this process differently. Any requirements are kept to a minimum and as few couples as possible are rejected. In this way, the birthparents have the widest choice possible. Counseling and educational sessions follow. These cover everything from how to prepare for becoming adoptive parents to the details of how to "network" to friends and family about their search for a child.

2. Birthparents usually find out about adoption through pregnancy counselors, doctors, and friends or often in response to listings in the yellow pages or advertising in newspapers or magazines. They are typically single and in their early twenties, though their ages can range from twelve years old to late thirties. About one-fifth of the birthfathers actively participate and often the birthmother's parents (the birthgrandparents) are helping her through the process. Counseling covers not only adoption but all other alternatives as well. The counselor or attorney assesses the birthparents' readiness to make an adoption decision and the support or opposition for their adoption choice by their friends and family. The birthmother is screened for possible drug use and possible legal complications are explored. The birthparents then make their initial choice of adopting parents for their child. Typically, they choose from a notebook containing

photos and letters from all the prospective adopting parents listed with the agency.

3. Once the birthparents have made their selection, the prospective adopting parents are told about the birthparents, the counselor's or attorney's assessment of their readiness for choosing to have their child adopted, and any unusual characteristic of the adoption such as exceptionally high costs, special risks, and health problems. All parties are invited to meet with a trained counselor. When the birthparents and adopting parents meet, they are free to ask any questions of each other (and also free not to answer any questions). These questions usually cover why the adoptive parents want children, their plans for the future, and their child-rearing ideas. The birthparents are asked about their own life experiences especially related to their pregnancy and adoption choice. The counselor meets with all parties individually, both before and after this 'match' meeting, to help all parties decide if this is the right situation for them. After a 24 hour 'waiting' period, the adoptive parents and birthparents make their final decision.

4. Counseling is offered on a regular basis to the birthmother and birthfather, the birthgrandparents, and any other party involved in the birthparents' life. Support is also provided to the adopting parents and their families including their children and parents. This counseling may be in the form of individual counseling, group sessions, or peer counseling with other birthparents or adopting parents. In many fully open adoption programs, some form of "Open Adoption Agreement" is worked out between the adopting and birthparents with the help of the counselors. This specifies how the logistics of their relationship will be handled including what will happen at the hospital, how and when pictures and letters will be exchanged, and the plans for future visits by the birthparents to the new adoptive family. While adoption information is kept private (in terms of the public at large), all important information is shared between the adoptive parents and birthparents.

5. To the extent allowed by a state's laws on adoptions, the adopting couple pays the birthmother's expenses but only those expenses specifically incurred by her and directly related to the pregnancy. This can include medical, legal, counseling, and special foods for the pregnancy. The birthmother and birthfather cannot receive any money for the child beyond pregnancy expenses. Private adoption practitioners cannot receive any funds for finding the child for the adoptive parents, only for their legal and counseling services.

6. At the hospital, the adopting parents are often in the room for the birth or close at hand. At the appropriate point, in most open adoptions, the birthparents personally give the child to their new parents.

7. Exactly how the adoption is legally finalized depends on whether an agency or a private practitioner facilitates the adoption. With an agency adoption, the adoptive parents have been screened and certified beforehand. The agency is licensed by the state and is therefore granted considerable power over the adoption process. For instance, there is usually only a very brief period in which the birthparents can change their mind in an agency adoption. Typically, this ranges from 24 hours to a few weeks. Once the agency's 'relinquishment' or 'surrender' document is signed by the birthmother, the adoption is virtually irrevocable. Issues about birthfathers also have to be resolved but are often completed before the birth. In attorney adoption, the legal situation is different. Generally, a state agency screens the adoptive parents sometime after, not before, the birth. The birthparents usually have anywhere from 30 to 45 working days to change their mind about the adoption and, in some cases, up to six months or more to do so.

Once the adoption is finalized, the hospital issues a new birth certificate for the child with only the names of the adopting parents and child and the original date of birth. The original birth certificate is either destroyed or sealed.

8. Because this is so important to the adoptive child, typically there is some form of ongoing relationship between the adoptive family and the birthparents. The nature and frequency of that relationship is based on mutually acceptable decisions made by the adoptive parents and birthparents. Typically, there are a number of visits by the birthparents during the first year of the child's life. In later years, the contact is often less frequent.

1

Why Is Adopting a Healthy Infant So Difficult?

*T*hirty or forty years ago, almost anyone could walk into an adoption agency and find a baby to adopt. There were more children available than there were couples to adopt them. Because homes could not be found for all the children, orphanages were common. What a contrast to the situation today where there are an estimated forty to a hundred couples wanting to adopt for every adoptable child.[1] What happened to all those unwanted babies? Why has adoption become so difficult?

Part of the problem is the increase in infertility. Just a few generations ago, perhaps only one in a hundred couples had a difficult time conceiving a child. The cause of their difficulty was usually not a specific infertility disorder, but the result of a more general health problem such as a chronic illness or a war wound. But infertility has increased dramatically in the last ten to twenty years. Most often the problem lies in getting pregnant. There are also other difficulties such as multiple miscarriages, medical or genetic risks with pregnancy or childbirth, and voluntary sterilization in a previous marriage. All in all, today somewhere between one in six and one in five couples of childbearing age have serious problems bearing their own child.

Any health problem that affects that large a percentage of the population is serious. An epidemic is declared when an illness affects only 4 to 8 percent of a population. Infertility affects two or three times that percentage of people of childbearing age. Not only are the percentages high, but because of the population affected, the absolute numbers are even more extreme. Infertility is primarily a concern of people in their thirties to early forties; it is the "baby-boom" generation that is experiencing the greatest distress. Since that generation is the largest in number in American history, a 15 to 20 percent infertility rate means that literally millions of people are confronting the problem of bringing a child into their families.

As infertility has been rising, the number of babies available for adoption has been plummeting. A few generations ago, some 50 to 60 percent of unmarried, pregnant women chose to have their children adopted. Today, a million and a half young, single women do get pregnant each year but one third of these pregnancies are terminated by abortion and, in 96 percent of the remaining cases, the women keep their children, deciding in favor of single motherhood.[2] This leaves fewer than 3 percent of these single women choosing to have their children adopted. In other words, the dramatic increase in infertility has coincided with an equally dramatic decrease in the number of babies available for adoption. The timing could not have been more devastating for those millions of people wanting to adopt.

❖ If only my husband and I could have adopted years ago, we wouldn't still be waiting and waiting and waiting to find a baby. We could have gotten one in the old days when almost no one had infertility problems and there were more than enough babies to go around. We would be happy parents today. But instead, we are now one of so many millions of people looking for a baby and almost no babies out there to adopt. It just does not seem fair. It does not seem fair at all. Maybe this is a sign that we don't deserve to be parents anyway.

The reasons for the increase in infertility are unclear, are somewhat in dispute, and are beyond the scope of this book. But the virtual abandonment of adoption by young people can be explained. The fact is that the procedures for having a child adopted are a nightmare of red tape and humiliation, while the other alternatives, abortion and single parenting, have become relatively easy and socially acceptable.

Only a few generations ago, when a majority of unwed mothers had their babies adopted, there were few other choices. Abortion was illegal. Some women did have illegal abortions but most could not or would not take that risk. They worried about the consequences of getting caught and the poor quality of the medical procedures to which they had to submit themselves. Single parenting, on the other hand, was not yet a viable alternative in mainstream American life. The words single and parenting placed side by side were an oxymoron; the word *parents* meant a mother and a father, not a woman choosing to raise a child by herself. A young, pregnant, unmarried woman could give birth to her baby, but there was no question that she either had to get married or find someone to adopt the child. In some cases parents forced marriages, as in those movie scenes with the angry father and his shotgun forcing the young man to agree to marry his daughter. But that is in the movies; in real life, that alternative was often no more acceptable than abortion or the mother raising the child on her own. In the past, then, having a child adopted was by far the most workable and acceptable solution to an unwed pregnancy. Today, however, the situation has changed dramatically.

The More Appealing Alternatives: Abortion and Single Parenting

❖ As a sixteen year old, would I have an abortion if I were pregnant? Well, maybe.

Keep the child? You mean I'd be a mother instead of a teenage girl? Everybody would have to give me some respect. I would have this nice little baby and all my friends would help, I'm sure. And if I had to go on welfare? What is wrong with that? I could live on my own and be independent.

Have the baby adopted? You've got to be kidding. I wouldn't even think of doing that. I would rather die. The thought of it makes me want to throw up.

In the last twenty years, abortion has become a widely obtainable option for young women facing a pregnancy for which they are unprepared. Although some people consider abortion morally unacceptable, most regard it as a perhaps unfortunate but sometimes necessary step to resolve a difficult situation. The medical procedure itself takes only a few minutes, is rarely dangerous, and is usually available on an outpatient basis (in a clinic or doctor's office, instead of a hospital). The cost is low and often covered through a state medical program or personal health insurance. The abortion ends the pregnancy in its early stages, before it starts to have a serious effect on the young woman's schooling, work, or lifestyle.

Yet abortion is the solution in only one third of unwed pregnancies. The more frequent choice is single motherhood, an option almost unknown only a few decades ago. In the past, mothers without husbands were treated as promiscuous and low class. But in the 1960s and 1970s, a series of events changed this. The women's movement insisted that divorce was preferable to staying in an oppressive marriage even if there were children in the family. As the divorce rate began to accelerate, the number of single—meaning divorced—mothers increased. While in 1970 well over two thirds of American households consisted of married couples, by 1990 that percentage had fallen to just a little more than half.[3] With so many single mothers around, no one could tell the difference between a child who was born out of wedlock and a child whose mother simply no longer had a husband. Since divorce was common among the middle and upper classes, being an unwed mother could no longer be equated with poverty. Our society's attitude toward unmarried mothers shifted so radically that popular television family sitcoms were as likely to star a single mother (or father) as they were to portray the more traditional mom-and-dad combination. The TV show "Kate and Allie," for instance, shared first or second place in the ratings for years, and shows like "Who's the Boss" or "Designing Women" feature or star single parents.

This change in attitude toward single parents was and remains important to the millions of women (and men) who find themselves in this role because of divorce. Yet there is a considerable difference between a single mother who is a reasonably mature, stable, and financially secure thirty- to forty-year-old woman (or man) and a fifteen- to twenty-year-old single mother who has not even graduated from high school. Unfortunately, that distinction has gotten lost in our society's broad acceptance of single parenting. Through television, movies, even the offering of support programs in the schools for teen mothers, the message goes out to young people that single parenting is not only acceptable but even laudable, regardless of age, maturity, or financial ability to parent.

Single parenting is almost universally acceptable among

young people today. In the past, unwed motherhood brought expulsion from school and social ostracism. For many a young woman today, single motherhood is the ultimate symbol of being grown up. She is no longer a teenage girl but a mother. The welfare available to single mothers in most states is pathetic—typically around four hundred dollars or so a month for a woman and child. Yet for a young woman used to ten dollars a week allowance, four hundred dollars may sound like the promise of freedom and her chance to be independent from her parents.

It is not hard to see why adoption has such a hard time competing with abortion and single parenting. Generations ago, the woman, her child, and her family either pursued adoption or faced the lifelong shame of being labeled an unwed mother and illegitimate child. Today, with that pressure removed, adoption is not likely to be chosen as an alternative. Why should it be? Adoption offers no immediate gain: no change in status to mothers and no welfare payments. There are often social costs as well. There is tremendous peer pressure against choosing adoption. Men and women who turn to adoption are often verbally and even physically assaulted for their choice.[4] As if all this were not hard enough, deciding to have a child adopted is difficult right from the start. Compare adoption to abortion or single parenting. Certainly having an abortion can be a difficult decision, but the consequences seem limited: the pregnancy is usually terminated almost as soon as it begins. Likewise, taking the first step toward single parenting appears easy as well, even if the long-term consequences may be severe. The young woman does not have to do anything; she just has to stay pregnant. In contrast, putting a child up for adoption demands living through the entire pregnancy, going through the pains of childbirth, and then giving up the child for life.

The Pressures Against a Young Woman (and Man) Choosing Adoption

Could this society find ways to encourage young people at least to consider choosing adoption? Perhaps. We could emphasize how caring and responsible adoption can be, and how the choice can be an act of love toward themselves, toward the people who want a child so badly, and, most of all, toward their child. Few things annoy young people more than being told what to do, especially by older adults. Since that is the case, the decisions about what happens to their child in an adoption should be up to the birthmother and birthfather themselves, not bureaucrats and strangers. That seems only fair, anyway, since the child is their biological creation.

Unfortunately, the message of our society is just the opposite. For years books, movies, and TV shows have portrayed women who choose adoption as pathetic at best, and more often as heartless, cruel, and unloving.[5] Generally, adoption is treated as so unthinkable that it does not even deserve to be mentioned as an alternative. In 1988, for instance, both *Time* and *Newsweek* published major stories on the problems of teen pregnancy. Although the stories ran for dozens of pages, in neither issue was adoption given more than one or two lines, or a passing and obscure reference.[6] A widely read Congressional study on teen pregnancy in the 1980s followed the same course.[7] In most of the materials available for school, counseling, and medical personnel who work with young women, the situation is the same: only limited information on adoption is available. From an ethical and professional standpoint, no one should be forced into giving up a child for adoption, nor should counselors or medical personnel impose their values on their students or clients or patients. But the issue is not forcing someone into choosing adoption; the question is whether young people are aware that adoption is any alternative at all. A recent federal study showed that "pregnancy counselors failed to include adoption 40 percent of the time as an option during discussions with pregnant women, and 60 percent of the time, counselors mentioning adoption presented inaccurate facts concerning adoption."[8]

A few years ago, I pointed out to the leader of a large organization of teachers who worked with pregnant teens that their upcoming conference on school programs for pregnant adolescents included almost no workshops on adoption. His response was that the conference did not need to cover this issue since so few of their students ever chose adoption. The organization's attitude was a classic example of a self-fulfilling prophecy. If counselors and teachers expect only a few women to choose adoption and hence rarely discuss the matter with their students, this almost ensures that the number choosing adoption will remain minuscule.

The hostility toward adoption is pervasive even at the hospitals where the to-be-adopted children are born. Like other institutions, hospitals mirror society's dominant values and ideas. But hospitals, unlike many other institutions, often have to put these values down in writing, in the form of specific medical procedures and protocols. Almost every medical institution has such protocols for adoption. The two most common are referred to as the "Do Not Show" and "Do Not Publish" procedures, abbreviated DNS and DNP respectively. Whenever any woman enters a hospital to deliver a baby, there are standard intake routines to follow, vital signs to take, tests related to the pregnancy and birth to complete, and appropriate medical preparations for the hospital staff to make. But when a woman is planning to have her child adopted, there is an additional step. The letters DNS and DNP are written on her chart and all medical personnel are notified of her special status.

The Do Not Show protocol directs the staff to proceed with the birth in such a way as to ensure that the mother does not see the baby she is placing for adoption. In the past, this required only minor changes in the standard medical procedures. Since in most births, the mother was completely sedated, the birthmother needed only be given some extra anesthesia. In recent years, however, this process has become more difficult. Today, most doctors prefer the mother to be conscious throughout labor and delivery and the use of general anesthesia is discouraged. As a result, the traditional DNS procedure had to be changed. Typically, the new protocol prescribes that first the nurse prevent the birthmother from seeing the baby through the special mirror that's normally placed above the delivery table so that a new mother can see her baby being born. With the DNS protocol, the nurses or attendants usually cover this mirror with a towel or sheet. Moreover, as the baby's head starts to emerge, the doctor, nurse, or birth coach holds the mother's head up and back so she cannot look down and see the baby. Only once the baby is "safely" in another room is the birthmother allowed to put her head back down.

Certainly these procedures are not followed out of malice. They were developed out of the adoption professionals' belief that the birthmother would feel less grief—or would be less likely to change her mind—if she never saw her baby. Yet almost everything we have learned about the grief process in the last twenty years indicates that this is the wrong approach. Those who work in the field of grief therapy are almost unanimous in their findings that mourning is not a one-shot emotion but a long-term process with many different stages, each of which is necessary and important. The pain from the loss of a child, relative, or friend is not eliminated by trying to pretend the hurt never happened. The opposite seems the healthiest and most promising way to help people deal with grief: patient listening, caring support, and plenty of time to think about the loss. Many years ago, for instance, a mother and father who experienced the stillbirth and death of their baby were not allowed to see or touch the child, or even to arrange a funeral or bereavement ceremony. Today, in order to give parents the opportunity to work through their loss, most hospitals no longer deny these options. The same approach should apply to a mother facing the grief of giving her child up for life. But rarely is this the case.

The Do Not Publish protocol reflects the same demeaning attitude toward birthmothers. The letters DNP on a birthmother's chart instruct the medical staff that her presence at the hospital is to be kept secret at all times. There is to be no name on her door, no release of her phone number or room assignment to anyone calling or visiting. In fact, if anyone calls for her while she is in the hospital, they are usually told she is not there. Again, the intention is not malevolent; in this case, the hospital is just attempting to protect the birthmother from the stigma of unwed motherhood. But, as with the DNS protocol, the message is clear: these women must have done something terrible to deserve such treatment.

While these protocols are not universally followed, neither are they confined to remote areas of the country. A few years ago, I encountered the DNP protocol in a leading hospital in liberal northern California. At the time, the center was working with a wonderful young woman named Laura and her boyfriend, Michael. They were both in their early twenties and realized they were not prepared to be the type of parents they wanted to be. They had gone to a pregnancy counseling clinic and then been referred to our center. They were counseled about adoption alternatives and eventually picked a couple to adopt their baby, who was due in a few months. Late one night, about two months after the adoption arrangements were all in place, I was on call at the Adoption Center when Laura called. She said she thought she was in labor but did not want to go to the hospital yet. She had promised Mary and David, the adopting parents, that she would call them first so they could be there for the birth. But she could not reach them. She wanted to know what to do. Obviously, I told her to go right to the hospital and assured her that we would keep trying to find Mary and David for her. Laura and Michael went off to the hospital, and we finally did contact the adoptive parents. They were out of town, and when we told them what was happening, they went into a panic about returning for the birth. But there was simply no way they could get back until the next day. I assured them that everything would still be okay. I told them we would be sure to let Laura know that they would be there as soon as humanly possible and, of course, we would go see her and provide whatever support and counseling were needed.

I called the hospital early the next morning to talk to Laura and find out what was happening with the birth. When I asked for Laura by name, the hospital claimed they had never heard of any such person. I pointed out, to no avail, that I was calling Laura to connect her to professional counselors and that I wanted to be sure she received the support she needed, including important information about the whereabouts of the adopting parents. The hospital personnel still insisted there was no such woman at the hospital. We were outraged but did not give up, and finally managed to get in to see Laura many hours later. In a meeting with the hospital's top administrators a week later, I asked if they had received our letter about Laura and her choice of an open adoption. The letter was a standard correspondence the center sends out to medical centers stating that a birthmother is coming to their facility to have her child adopted. It goes on to explain that, since this is an open adoption, there is no need to be concerned about secrecy. The letter also offers the hospital the opportunity to call the counseling staff if they have any questions about open adoption. The administrator admitted receiving the letter but told us that they did not break their Do Not Publish protocol for anyone, anytime, no matter what the circumstances. This would be the case whether we had written permission from the adopting parents, the birthparents, or the doctor. When I asked to whom such a serious and rigid protocol applied, the administrator answered, "In cases involving knife wounds, gunshot wounds, suicide, drug overdoses, *and adoptions.*"

These hospital protocols, though shocking, are not the problem in themselves. Few people are even aware they exist. But they reflect the extraordinary insensitivity of our society toward the young people who make the difficult decision in favor of adoption. Not only must they resist their peers' pressure against this choice, but they also must face the strong possibility of mistreatment by professionals, not to mention society at large, for their decision. Ironically, our society might be able to get away with this shabby treatment of birthparents if these young women were fairly passive personalities or poorly educated. But, in fact, most of these women are the opposite: bright and mature. Who else would choose adoption over the easier options of abortion or young, single parenthood? But that also means that they are just the types of women (and men) who would most resent the control and humiliation characteristic of traditional adoption practices.

We might hope that state and private adoption agencies would be on the other side of this issue, that they would be in the forefront of countering these negative attitudes toward adoption. Unhappily, this has not been the case. The traditionally closed and secretive procedures of most agencies have only validated and reinforced the general social view that adoption is shameful. A few years ago, one agency social worker admitted to me that even during the 1960s, her agency often prescribed tranquilizers for their birthmothers to keep them from becoming too upset. Many adoption agencies have separate waiting rooms, entrances, and even parking lots for birthparents and adopting parents.[9] Supposedly, this is to ensure that the birthparents will not accidentally run into the adopting parents. What such procedures actually communicate to all parties is a feeling that birthparents are so frightening and strange that they have to be hidden from view. As one birthmother explained, "It's the adoption agencies' version of sending you to the back of the bus." Even supposedly neutral legal forms are insulting. In most states, especially on the East Coast, the formal paper signed by a birthparent to relinquish her child for adoption is called a "surrender" document. For many birthmothers, signing this paper makes them feel like criminals, as if a policeman were telling them to put up their hands and surrender their children.

Is it surprising that so few young people consider adoption when they are treated in this manner? Given how much easier and more acceptable are the other alternatives, it is astonishing that even 3 percent choose the adoption route. For decades now, when a young woman has called inquiring about adoption as an alternative for her baby, adoption agencies have responded with one or another version of "There, there, honey, you messed up badly, but now we will take care of absolutely everything for you." No wonder there are so few babies available for adoption.

Notes

1. Please note that I am talking here about healthy infants, not the shocking number of children—usually referred to as "hard-to-place" or "special needs" children—who are either emotionally or physically handicapped, and for whom it is difficult to find permanent homes. Sometimes people outside of the adoption world complain that infertile couples should just adopt one of these thousands of special needs children. Yet to adopt such a child requires a unique mental and financial commitment, along with solid previous experience with childrearing. These children deserve to be adopted by people who willingly and knowingly take on that responsibility and are not forced into the choice.

2. Allan Gutmacher Institute, *News*, 1985.

3. U.S. Census Bureau, quoted in *Newsweek*, April 11, 1991, p. 12.

4. Most of the birthmothers I have worked with at the center have been over twenty years old, but when we do have school-aged young women, we often recommend that they get a private tutor and drop out of school until the adoption is completed. Otherwise, they frequently face verbal and even physical harassment from their peers.

5. Consider, for instance, movies like *False Shame* (1964) and *The Baby Maker* (1960), and references to birthmothers in a variety of soap operas. In recent years, films like *Immediate Family* (1988) and

television shows like "LA Law" have portrayed birthmothers some-what more sympathetically, but they are the exception.

6. "Children Having Children: Teenage Pregnancy in America," *Time*, December 9, 1985, and "Life with Two Mothers," *Newsweek*, May 12, 1986.

7. "Teen Pregnancy: What Is Being Done: A State-by-State Look," U.S. Congressional Report, House Select Committee on Children and Families.

8. Study conducted by the U.S. Department of Health and Human Services, 1989, as reported in "Review and Outlook: The Adoption Outlook," *The Wall Street Journal*, July 7, 1989, p. 21.

9. A separate waiting room is still required by California adoption regulations.

2

Open Adoption: The Revitalization of Adoption

*D*rastic changes were needed if adoption was to be revitalized for the sake of birthparents, adopting parents, and society as a whole. Fortunately, in the last ten to fifteen years, new, more open procedures have emerged aimed at correcting the problems created by traditional closed adoption. The advocates of open adoption argued that more young people would consider adoption if the process were more loving, caring, and above all, respectful of the birthparents' rights and concerns. And they were right. Today, open adoption is making adoption an alternative to abortion or single parenting. With more young people choosing this option, there is also new hope for people looking to adoption to bring the joy of parenting into their lives.

But if closed adoption was such a problem, why did it

dominate adoption for so long? Why has open adoption emerged as such a strong alternative in recent years?

The Origins of Closed Adoption

Closed adoption procedures were born in the late nineteenth century. At the time, a strong social reform movement sought protection and help for unwed pregnant women and their illegitimate children through the founding of state-licensed adoption agencies. There were two central issues about how these programs should be administered. First, who determined who adopted which baby? In the democratic tradition, biological parents have certain fundamental rights concerning their children. But, in the eyes of nineteenth-century society, the birthmother forfeited that right because of her presumed promiscuity. The founders of the first adoption agencies felt compassion for the plight of unwed mothers but still considered them sinners and social outcasts. The other party to the adoption—the adopting parents—might have been consulted about the placement of the children, but they, too, were social pariahs. After all, they were barren and, in those days at least, their infertility was seen as the result of being cursed by God. The children themselves were too young to have any say. Only the agency's own social workers had the legitimacy and social standing to make the critical decisions in each adoption. Given the social milieu of the day, adoption agencies met little resistance establishing their almost total power over the adoption process.[1]

The second issue concerned secrecy: should some or all information about the adopting parents, birthparents, and the adopted child be kept hidden? Given the shame associated with adoption in those days, secrecy seemed both kind and mandatory. Yet there was some resistance to this type of secretive approach to adoption. After all, as a democratic country, the United States has had a proud tradition of being distrustful of any type of governmental secrecy. This has been the case from the Founding Fathers and the Bill of Rights to the Watergate scandal and the dispute over media access to information in the 1991 Gulf War. Because of this opposition, some laws requiring secrecy in adoption were not approved until the 1940s. But soon they were part of every state's regulations concerning adoption.

With closed adoption, neither birthparents nor adopting parents were permitted access to any information about each other. Information on their biological origins was kept from adopted children even when they reached adulthood. While such clandestine procedures seem shocking today, they probably served an important function in their day. The secrecy protected the birthmother from being labeled a fallen woman and facing a lifetime of social ostracism. Adoption shielded the child from being branded illegitimate. In many states, hospitals routinely stamped the birth certificate of a child born to an unwed mother with the word *illegitimate* printed in large red letters. But once the child was adopted, the court replaced this stigmatized birth certificate with a more conventional version that made no reference to the child's biological parents, married or unmarried.

For all of these reasons, "closed adoption" became synonymous with "adoption" by the middle of the twentieth century. Regulations forbade any exchange of information between adopting parents and birthparents and all adoption records were sealed. All control over the adoption process was taken from birthparents and entrusted solely to licensed agencies.

The Problems with Closed Adoption

Closed adoption advocates may have been well meaning but their procedures often created serious hardships. Most worrisome was the effect on the adopted children themselves. Many paid a high price for the secrecy surrounding their closed adoption.

A striking number of children and adults who were adopted through closed adoption experience serious emotional and psychological problems.[2] One explanation is that the adopted child does not know his or her own family history, something most people take for granted. The average person knows the identity of his or her siblings, parents, aunts, uncles, nieces, nephews, and grandparents. People know their national and racial origins and sometimes their family history far into the past. That seemingly basic information is not part of an adopted child's heritage. This can lead to what sociologists and psychologists sometimes call genealogical bewilderment.[3]

❖ I was adopted through a closed adoption and I really missed not having a sense of history. I don't think people realized how much that means to you. Somebody would come up to me and tell me that they were Irish, or Indian Irish, English Irish, and I couldn't say anything back. I know my son Michael [his adopted son through an open adoption] will never feel that way. He will know his birthmother and he will know why she gave him up for adoption and he also will have that history.

What happens in a closed adoption when a child asks about his or her biological background?[4] Sometimes children do not ask this question until they are ten or twelve years old, but often this issue comes up at an earlier age. Because of the secrecy of traditional adoption, the parent's answer has been "I don't know" or "I cannot tell you." The impact of that response can be harsh for both child and parent. The problem

is more than the absence of information. Even more important
for the child is the question of why this information is being
withheld. There is an association in our society between secrecy and shame. We associate secrecy with dirty dealing,
with the Mafia, or with espionage. We talk openly and freely
about information of which we are proud or, at least, have
neutral feelings. Children do not have to be very old to figure
out that if information about their adoption is being withheld
from them, then it must be a terrible story indeed. As a result,
they may carry throughout their lives the suspicion that the
lack of information about their birth suggests a terrible past
and an embarrassing biological origin.

> ❖ "Was she some kind of prostitute or something? Was
> he a criminal or something? Did they just leave me in a
> trashcan somewhere?" asked our son Marty, an adopted
> child of eleven.
>
> "No, of course not. Your mother and I are sure they
> were both fine people," we answered.
>
> "If they were such fine people, then how come you
> can't tell me about them? If they were so okay, then you
> would know the story. Is it so terrible that you just don't
> want to tell me?" he responded.
>
> "No, no! We just don't know the details," we valiantly
> tried to explain.
>
> "Oh, sure!" he said, in that disbelieving tone a child
> can use so effectively.

Some children handle this secrecy by never asking again
and some, by asking repeatedly. Sometimes adopted children
pretend that their biological parents were kings and queens
or famous movie stars. Typically, this is a defense mechanism
to cover their fear that their biological parents were shameful
people. Such defense mechanisms do not always work; un-
derneath, the child may still feel shame about the people who
brought him or her into the world.

Equally destructive to adopted children is their concern

about why their biological parents chose to have them adopted. Many come to believe that their birthparents placed them for adoption because they, as babies, were ugly, despised, or hated. If they were not so bad, and if their first mother (or father) loved them, how could their biological parents have just walked away and never looked back? Why didn't their birthparents ever try to find out what had happened to their child?

❖ Our son Jimmy was adopted six years ago in a private attorney adoption but we were not allowed to meet or exchange any information with the birthparents. We did know, though, which city the birthmother lived in and often drove through that same town. When we did, we would occasionally say to Jimmy that this was where his birthmother had lived. Usually he would just nod his head and not say anything. Then one day, as we drove through that town once again, Jimmy turned to us and said, "Why didn't my first mommy even say good-bye?"

❖ My husband and I adopted our first daughter, Stacy, thirteen years ago. Before Stacy's adoption, our opinion of her birthparents was ill-defined. Our fantasies about these people ranged from the mother being a fertile but uncaring woman and the father being an irresponsible cad to them both being indecisive about their decision to place Stacy. Our worst fear is that they would become villainous kidnappers who would one day reappear to claim her.

Our fantasies about Stacy's birthparents were not lessened by the circumstances of her adoption. Stacy's placement with us was closed. We lived on with ill-founded ideas about Stacy's birthmother, as her birthmother undoubtedly lived with incorrect assumptions about herself.

Opening her adoption became necessary for Stacy

soon after her eighth birthday. On the morning of her special day, my husband and I found her in tears before her bathroom mirror. "My birthmother gave me away because she is blond and I am not." The depth of her despair tore at our hearts. How could such a beautiful dark-haired girl believe she was rejected because of her looks?[5]

With closed adoption, there were also problems for the adoptive parents, not just the adopted child. Imagine how Jimmy's parents felt in the example above. The pain of seeing their child hurt by the secrecy around his or her adoption and being helpless to do anything about it can be devastating to an adopting parent.

❖ When I adopted my daughter fifteen years ago, it seemed so easy. I just walked into a room and they handed her to me. She had been born six days before. I did not have to deal with any birthparents or any complications like that. It was easy. Or so I thought until five years later when my daughter asked me, "Why did my first mommy throw me away?" She was in terrible pain but so was I, about what had I done to my daughter.

Proponents of closed adoption assumed that connections between adopting parents and birthparents were neither desirable nor possible. Adopting couples, agencies felt, would be too scared, and the birthmothers too weak for such contact. So, instead of helping everyone overcome their fears and understand and appreciate each other, the agencies insisted on secrecy and forbade any contact. These policies not only failed to help but, instead, reinforced the fears of the adopting parents about their child's birthparents. Why did the agency insist on hiding the birthparents' identity so carefully, the adopting couples sometimes wondered. What were they hiding? Was there something wrong about the adoption or with them as adoptive parents? Was there some dreadful secret about the birthparents?

Another aspect of closed adoption was equally destructive, though in a more subtle way. In closed adoption, the biological parents do not, personally, give the child to the adopting parents. Instead, this is handled by an intermediary: a doctor, lawyer, or social worker. Because the child is not handed to them by the birthparents, the process sometimes feels "unnatural." At times, this can deepen the doubts adopting parents already have about their legitimacy as parents.

> ❖ I remember walking into the room and having the social worker hand me my adopted baby. I knew that was what was going to happen but suddenly I realized that this was not my picture of how you got a baby. Having a baby was a wonderful event, not something done behind closed doors. Being handed a child, in a closed room by a stranger instead of by a woman who bore him, seemed wrong. Although I knew everything was completely on the up-and-up, I still felt more like I was stealing a baby than becoming a parent. Of course, I took little Danny and I have no regrets about that, but still I wondered if there was not some better way.

Most people mistakenly assume that far fewer birthmothers change their minds in closed adoptions than in open adoptions. After all, the process is carefully controlled by the agency and all information is kept from the birthparents. In fact, though, many birthmothers do change their minds in closed adoption programs, but the collapse of these adoptions is hidden from public view by the very secrecy of the process. The most common problem in these cases is the absence of any relationship between the adopting parents and birthparents that is inherent in closed adoptions. When a birthmother experiences the intense sense of loss and grief that can accompany giving up a child, she has little to counterbalance that pain in a closed adoption. After all, her commitment to follow through with the adoption has been made only to an institution. She has no connection to any real, live adopting parents whom she has met and personally chosen to parent her child. Since she does not know the adopting parents, she also does not experience firsthand their excitement about finally having a baby and their gratitude for her gift. The very separation that closed adoption supposedly uses to protect the adopting parents can result in their having no baby to adopt at all.

For birthparents, closed adoption can be a nightmare. They can never be sure their child is happy or even alive. They can not visualize their child being with a nice family because they knew nothing of the adopting parents. Many birthmothers have been so traumatized by the closed adoption process that they never become parents themselves. For many, the pain is intense and lasts a lifetime.[6]

❖ I am twenty-eight years old, married, and raising my one-year-old son. Six years ago, though, in a closed adoption, I gave a child up through an attorney and no one told me anything about the adopting parents. All I knew was that they were from the Modesto, California, area. One day recently, I picked up the local newspaper and read one of those horrifying stories of child abuse. But this particular story was about a six-year-old living with his parents in Modesto. Immediately my mind began to spin. The article also mentioned that the child was adopted. Could this be the child I had brought into the world? I had no way of knowing. Granted, the odds were against it but I could not be sure. Even today, I still do not know the truth about it all.

❖ When I was a teenager I got a girl pregnant. We got married but knew we were not ready to be parents. This was in the days when abortion was illegal so we gave the child up for adoption. It was one of those closed adoptions where the baby pops out and they take it away and you never see it again.

I saw Cheri, my ex-wife, the other day for the first time in several years. I found out she has been looking for this girl for twenty years. After Cheri turned eighteen, she took the first $5,000 that she earned and hired a private detective to try to find the baby, but the detective disappeared with the money. Then somebody else took her money and never came through with anything. She has had an awful time of it.

Recently, my new wife and I adopted a child. I almost did not want to tell Cheri. I was afraid she would be upset. Our adoption was an open adoption and our birthmother will never have to face all the pain Cheri has had to endure. When I finally told her, Cheri seemed happy that at least this is working out for us. Yet I don't think she will ever give up trying to find that girl.

The Move to Open Adoption

*T*he underpinnings of closed adoption began to crumble by the 1960s and 1970s and the pressure for change began to mount. The use of secrecy to protect the adopted child seemed increasingly irrelevant as the term illegitimate almost disappeared from our language. Although calling a child a bastard was once a serious accusation, the word has become an anachronism, or used only in jest or anger. In most states, the term lacks validity in any legal proceedings. If a person's will leaves property to a legitimate child and not an illegitimate child, it is likely to be ruled invalid. Nor is secrecy needed any longer to protect the birthmother. Fewer and fewer young people worry about being called an unwed mother. Society and their peers simply call them by the neutral term single mother.

The number of young women placing a child for adoption through conventional agencies also plummeted. Young women simply were not willing to tolerate the patronizing, or more typically, insulting, attitude that is almost inherent in closed adoption. When adoption was the sole alternative to a lifetime of shame, a birthmother had little choice but to accept such treatment. But as the social mores against unwed motherhood disappeared, so did young people's tolerance of these attitudes. The women's movement reinforced these feelings with its insistence that women, young and old, be treated with respect and equality. As a result, homes for unwed mothers closed around the country. Some agencies informally gave up their infant placement programs altogether and, instead, focused on the acute need to find homes for children with special needs. The number of healthy infants available for adoption decreased every year. The failure of closed adoption often meant seven- to ten-year waits for couples wanting to adopt a baby.

Prospective adopting couples rebelled as well. They found the long wait for a child, now common with traditional agencies, to be intolerable. Nor were they willing to be treated as barren and therefore suspect. Our society's better understanding of health-related issues made clear that their infertility was a medical, not moral, problem. The agencies' often arbitrary criteria for acceptance soon became a source of annoyance. No one did home studies on biological parents; why were they required for adoptive parents? Weren't adoptive parents more likely to be good parents than some biological parents, who often became parents accidentally or on a whim? Most prospective adopting parents were older and more settled and had shown unusual determination by pursuing first difficult infertility treatments and then adoption. But the agencies did not listen. In fact, they took the opposite course.

Agencies had always claimed the right to judge who would be the best parents. The shortage of infants encouraged them to develop even more stringent requirements. They rejected applicants because they were over thirty-five years of age or might be when the adoption finally happened. Couples often found themselves at the mercy of a particular social worker's personal beliefs about parenting, such as the notion that divorced people could never be good parents. Many agencies excluded applicants who had already had children either in their current marriage or through a previous marriage. Most of these criteria were not only arbitrary but sadly out of touch with the norms of contemporary American society. In the last decade, there has been a virtual baby boom among fertile people in the very categories that agencies considered risky: men and women over thirty-five years of age, previously married men and women, and couples with children from earlier marriages.

Even the general social milieu of the last few decades mitigated against closed adoption. The secrecy and bureaucratic control in traditional adoption seemed out of place in the world of the feminist movement and the general cultural awakening of the period. Adults who were adopted as children started fighting back and demanding the right to know their personal histories. Birthmothers from past years started clamoring for change. Just as other nontraditional alternatives have emerged in the past two decades, so too did open adoption.

The initial push for open adoption came with the publication of *The Adoption Triangle* by A. D. Sorosky, Annette Baran, and Reuben Pannor in 1978. The authors, all social workers and therapists, told story after story of the destructiveness of closed adoption. They even implied that closed adoption was a form of child abuse. One of the first institutionalized open adoption programs began in Texas in 1978. Lutheran Social Services of Texas under Kathleen Silber and our own Independent Adoption Center began in 1982. By the late 1980s, there were several other open adoption programs in operation across the country and, in 1990, a nationwide organization, the National Federation for Open Adoption Education, was founded.

Today, as open forms of adoption have become more widely available, more and more young people see adoption as a possible alternative to abortion or single parenting. A study of 430 young women found that the opportunity for choosing an adoptive family, meeting them, and receiving updates about the baby doubled the number of young women who said they would consider adoption as an alternative.[7] In a recent study of nearly one thousand adoptions, the overwhelming majority of birthparents—especially birthmothers—were emphatic that, if their only choice were closed adoption, they would either have had an abortion or kept the child.[8]

❖ I personally couldn't imagine giving up Sam [her birthchild] in a closed adoption. I just couldn't always be wondering where he was, what kind of parents he was with, and what the home in which he was living was like. If I saw a couple with a newborn baby, I would wonder if that could be my baby, since I would never have seen him.

❖ As a birthgrandmother, I know that if Katherine, my daughter, had gone through a closed adoption, she would have changed her mind at the birth of her child. She could not have done it. If we had not known Mark and Jane [the adopting parents in her open adoption], if they had not been there at the birth, and if we hadn't known exactly where the baby was going and the kind of people who were taking her, Katherine just could not have given that child up. We could choose adoption for the baby only because we knew the people and knew the family.

An informal study of five hundred high school students compared the appeal of various adoption alternatives to young women if they were to face a crisis pregnancy.[9] Four times as many women said they would at least consider adoption if an open adoption program were available to them as opposed to only traditional adoption alternatives. As a result, most open adoption programs find they can now help couples adopt a child in a relatively short time.

Is Open Adoption a New Social Experiment?

*I*n a society that values freedom and democracy as ours does, closed and secretive programs, not open procedures, would seem to be the aberration. Built into the founding principles of the country and reinforced throughout our lives, openness is the norm and secretiveness the exception.

A few years ago, two nationally syndicated columnists, Ann Landers and Carl Rowan, attacked open adoption as an aberrant social experiment similar to open marriage.[10] Adoptive parents flooded them with mail including these letters from two mothers who had adopted children through an open adoption.

Dear Ann Landers,

I was furious after reading Carl Rowan's uninformed putdown of open adoption. I hope you will give equal time to someone who has actually experienced being an adoptive parent.

The adoptive child knows the people who are raising him are his parents, and that there are other special people in his life—among them, his birthparents. But Mr. Rowan announces that just seeing these people puts the child in limbo. This is a stinging invalidation of all adoptive parenting. He is suggesting that the bonds of adoption are not strong enough to stand up in comparison when biology walks through the door. (A common prejudice!)

To suggest a connection between open adoption and open marriage boils down to putting an important, loving relationship in the same league with an arrangement based on easy morals and self-deception.

There are enough misconceptions about adoption. I would appreciate it if you and Mr. Rowan would stop perpetuating them.

Sincerely,
Jill McCoy (A Real Mom)

Dear Ann:

In closed adoption, children grow up with two painful, gnawing questions: who do I look like, and why was I given up? Caitlin will grow up knowing where she got her sparkling blue eyes, and knowing what boundless love and courage went into Linda's decision. Just as important, Linda will not agonize throughout her life not knowing what became of her firstborn and always fearing the worst.

Open adoption is really normalized adoption, without secrets, fears, and shame. Surely the movement by adult adoptees to open closed adoption records shows that there is a problem with that approach.

Ann, for pregnant women who would consider adoption if they had some choices in the process, and in honor of birthmothers and the families they've helped create, please reconsider your position! I am proud to sign my name to this letter.

Pam Quillin

In many ways, open adoption is not even that new. Before the advent of licensed, and closed, adoption agencies, most traditional adoptions were characterized by a high degree of openness. Until the late nineteenth century in this country—and still today in much of the world—almost all adoptions were handled informally and unofficially. There were no agencies, counselors, doctors, or private attorneys involved in the process; it was a private, family matter. If a young woman was pregnant out of wedlock, her parents made arrangements for the baby's adoption with the help of the head of her extended family. Someone—an aunt or uncle, a brother or sister, a niece or nephew, a grandparent—became the parent of the child. No one filed any legal papers. Perhaps the child called the adopting parents aunt and uncle, but everyone knew they were the child's adopted parents. Such adoptions were commonplace. For instance, in *The Wizard of Oz*—among the most famous stories about home and family in America—the heroine, Dorothy, is an adopted child. She is being raised by her Auntie Em and Uncle Henry. When L. Frank Baum wrote the Oz books, this type of adoption was so common that no one considered that aspect of the story unusual or noteworthy.

Of course, these adoptions were handled within people's own families, while today's open adoptions usually involve people not related to each other. But the point is that in these truly traditional adoptions, people took for granted most of what we consider so new about today's open adoptions. For instance, one supposed innovation with open adoption is that the birthparents and adopting parents know each other's identities. Yet in preagency days, the adopting parents and birthparents almost always knew each other well: they were usually either related or, if not, were members of the same close community. With contemporary open adoption, adopting parents often keep the child's birthparents informed over the years about the child's health and general well-being. In the old days, because of relatives or proximity, the birthmother always had access to such information about the child. Before the coming of closed, agency adoption, most people would not even have considered having a child adopted by anyone except someone in their family or community of closest friends. Giving a child to, or adopting a child from, a stranger was simply unacceptable. In many ways, open adoption returns us to this more humane tradition.

Every generation and every society define for themselves what is normal. Years ago, most Western societies believed that only parents could choose the right spouse for their children. Prearranged marriages—where the bride and the groom might not even have met before the wedding—were the norm. Today, we regard such an arrangement as abnormal, unacceptable, and anachronistic. Within the next ten years, we may well come to think of closed adoption in the same way.

Darlene and Larry Cerletti's Story

What is it like to go through an open adoption? The rest of this book explores that question in detail. But here, let me share a concrete adoption story—the personal account of Larry and Darlene Cerletti[11]—as a general overview of the process.

> We were in our late thirties when we became interested in open adoption. We had been married almost twenty years. Our infertility had been a nightmare. First there were several miscarriages and then my last pregnancy lasted five and one half months and I delivered twin boys who only lived a day. We kept trying and that was when we found out that I had endometriosis. As time went on, all our friends got pregnant without any problems and I started to wonder why this was happening to me. We thought we were the only couple in the world who was going through these problems. Finally, we just gave up and decided that we were going to be childless.
>
> Then, in the summer of 1989, our dentist, of all people, asked why we did not have any children. We knew him quite well so we told him our story. He asked us why we didn't just adopt a baby. When we told him that there

just were no babies, he said that was nonsense. He and his wife took us out to dinner and told us that their two children were adopted. Larry and I were skeptical, but we thought we should at least check it out.

We went to an orientation program about open adoption in October 1989. We listened and thought that this couldn't be for real. How could we be expected to go through an adoption like that? We would have to keep in touch with a birthmother and a birthfather, and then have them as part of our family? We thought this was crazy and that there was no way it would ever work for us. Whoever heard of such a thing! There had been other adoptions in our family, but they were all private. We both come from local Italian families, and yes, they are warm and they welcome everyone. But they usually let everybody in through marriage or because they are friends of family, not because they are related through an adoption.

We listened but we didn't sign up. Instead, we went home and talked about it. Larry and I thought about it a lot and finally we decided to do it but on our own terms. We would send all our letters out of state and just would not accept a birthmother from anywhere around here. We could fly our birthmother here to have the baby, then fly her back home, and get rid of her. We would say thank you, you have made our dreams come true, and we will send you a picture once a year.

We called our parents and told them what we were going to do. They didn't like the idea at all. They thought of all the negative things—the birthparents would know where we lived, they might camp on our doorstep, and we might never get rid of them. Worse, they might even try to kidnap the baby. They were opposed to us trying an open adoption because they had seen us go through so much pain and they thought the whole thing was too high a risk. We wanted to do it anyway.

We called and made an appointment to meet with a counselor to work on our letter. She gave us samples of letters other couples had written to birthmothers. Then she told us to go home and write our own letter and take pictures. Well, Larry and I had been married a long time and, yes, we had our share of disagreements. But we almost got divorced over writing that letter and selecting the picture. He was sure he knew what a sixteen-year-old girl would expect out of a letter. I said that I had been a sixteen-year-old girl myself once, and that I knew what to write in the letter better than he did. Somehow we came up with what we thought was the perfect letter and took it back to our counselor. She took one look at it and we felt like we were back in English 1A again. She put red slash marks here, added words there, reversed this and punctuated that. Larry couldn't believe what she was doing. We finally got our letter done and it really was better than the original.

After that, we went to a number of open adoption workshops. We heard more about open adoption and heard more personal stories from adopting couples and even birthmothers. Clearly open adoption was right but, in our hearts, we were still not sure that it was right for *us*. Anyway, after going through the first workshop, we got to know the other adopting couples. We listened while they explained their experiences and fears and we realized that they were the same as ours. At the last workshop, I heard two of the couples behind me talking. The first one said that they had bought the bumper pads for their crib and the other one said that they put up wallpaper in the baby's room. I turned around and said I thought it was wonderful that they had already been matched with a birthmother. They told me that they weren't matched yet, but were just getting the rooms ready in advance. I told them I couldn't believe that they were doing that. Our baby room was still the guest room and I told them I was not going to worry about all that until we got a baby.

Only a few weeks later, I met our birthmother. She wanted to meet me right away so, even though Larry could not be there, I went to meet with her and the counselor. As soon as I met Noelle, I began to relax. She was so scared and so nervous that the motherly instinct in me just took over and I started mothering her. Kathleen said she would just let us talk for a while and get to know each other. I started by asking if she had finished high school. She looked at me and said she was twenty-five years old, had two years of college, and planned on going back to school after the baby was born. I said I was sorry and thought, Oh God, I've said the wrong thing already. There I was looking at the ground trying to figure out what to say. So I asked her if she had about three more months to go before she delivered. She said she was due next week. I thought, next week! Wait a minute here, our den is still the den and our guest room is still the guest room. What do you mean, you're due next week? But we had a really good talk, and she seemed certain that she was making the right decision. Then the counselor came back in and asked if Larry and I could get together the next day with Noelle to have our match meeting. I said yes and all the arrangements were made.

At the match, we spent about two hours talking together. Noelle spent time with Larry and me, then with the counselor, and then all of us met together. Noelle originally lived in Oregon with the birthfather. When she first suspected that she was pregnant, she just pretended it was not happening. After all, she had been taking her pills and therefore she couldn't be pregnant. She finally went to a doctor at three months and he confirmed that she was pregnant. Since she and the birthfather had planned to be married, she went back to tell him that she was pregnant and expected his total support. Instead, he looked at her and asked her who the father was. It was just like he had stuck a knife right through her.

Noelle wanted a mom and a dad for her baby so she called several different attorneys and looked into closed adoption. But they made it seem so formal and businesslike. The attorneys would tell her that they had very good couples and that she wouldn't have to worry about a thing. They would take the baby and if she wanted the adopting couple's address to write them that was fine, but there would be no further contact. But Noelle did not want it that way. A few weeks later, she heard about open adoption while watching a TV show. She knew right away that this was the alternative for her. She located an open adoption program and the rest is now history.

The day after meeting her, on Thursday morning, Larry went off to work and I went off to have my hair done. While I was there, Larry called and said to get home right away because Noelle was having the baby and wanted us in the delivery room. When we got to the hospital we went to the maternity floor. The nurses directed us to Noelle's room and we went in. Noelle had an IV hooked up and we went up and gave her a big hug and kiss and asked how she was doing. She said she was doing great. I asked if she was comfortable and she said she was. I told Noelle she was remarkable: Here you are delivering a baby and you are so calm. She replied, "Didn't anybody tell you, you have a son. He was born half an hour ago." I just started crying. Larry was right there but somehow I ran over to Noelle's mother though I had just met her for the first time. The nurse brought the baby in with this little blue hat on and asked everyone who was going to hold him. Noelle pointed at us and said that we were his mom and dad. I didn't think I could take him because I was such a mess, but Larry said that he was the father and he would hold him. I was just crying, I couldn't believe it. After I calmed down, Larry brought the baby to me and I held him. It was just such a wonderful moment. We brought our son Joey home the next day.

When we started with open adoption, we didn't even want to know the birthmother. Now she has turned out to be better than some of our own family members. Noelle has been our great treasure and strongest support. She says that she thanks God every day that she doesn't have to worry about her son. She calls us on the phone and we talk about everything and anything. We don't just talk about Joey. Once, when she didn't ask about Joey, I asked her if she was trying to forget him and get on with her life. She said that she didn't want us to think bad of her, but that she had picked us to be his parents. She knew that we were doing a fine job and didn't have to worry about him. I thought that was great and we went on talking about other things like gardening and decorating. We have a really good ongoing relationship. She doesn't call me every five minutes. In fact, Larry and I are usually the ones who call Noelle.

Noelle doesn't want to be called birthmother or mother, she wants to be called Noelle. I point out her photo to Joey in our adoption scrapbook but he doesn't understand yet. He is still too young, but I'm sure that, in time, he will know who she is. I'm just sorry that he won't know who his birthfather is. We are really sorry about that. We wish we could get in touch with him, but he is nowhere to be found.

Oh, one more thing. The day that Joey was born, the nurse came in and asked if we had picked out a name yet. We hadn't thought about it at all, so I asked Noelle if she had a name. She said that we were his parents and it was up to us. Then, she said, "I don't want to hurt your feelings, but I know you are Italian, and I just hope you don't name him Guido." Larry said that that was the name we had always wanted for our son, but he was just kidding, of course. Seriously, we asked her about Joseph Angelo for his name and she said that she liked that very much: St. Joseph was her patron saint.

That is our story. It's a wonderful story. It's a Cinderella story and we want to do it again.

Notes

1. More conservative forces thought that adoption agencies were making life too easy for unwed mothers who were, after all, such terrible people. Even today, some extremists in the so-called moral majority movement feel the same way about open adoption.

2. A. D. Soroksy, Annette Baran, and Reuben Pannor, *The Adoption Triangle* (New York: Anchor Books, 1978).

3. *Ibid.*

4. Years ago, many people never told their children they were adopted. Since the 1940s and 1950s, though, parents have been concerned that withholding this information was too great a risk to their child's well-being. If their child found out later in life that he or she was adopted, the anger and depression could be devastating. This issue was settled once and for all by Dr. Spock. In the 1950s, Dr. Spock's books became virtual bibles on childrearing, and adoptive parents heeded his clear advice to tell children at an early age that they were adopted.

5. Quoted in Kathleen Silber and Phyllis Speedlin, *Dear Birthmother* (San Antonio: Corona Publishing Company, 1991).

6. *The Adoption Triangle, op. cit.*

7. Debra Kalmus, Pearila Brickner Namerov and Linda Cushman, "Adoption Versus Parenting Among Young Pregnant Women," *Family Planning Perspectives*, Volume 23, Number 1, January/February 1991.

8. An unpublished study conducted by the Independent Adoption Center in 1988.

9. A unpublished study conducted in 1987 by the Adoption Education Project of the Independent Adoption Center.

10. "Case Closed on Open Adoption," Ann Landers, *Sacramento Bee*, Thursday, March 22, 1990, p. F2.

11. Unlike in most of the accounts in this book, the names Larry and Darlene Cerletti are the actual names of the adopting parents. Since this story is so detailed, I asked Larry and Darlene if I could use their names and they agreed. The birthmother's name, however, has been changed to protect her privacy.

3

Infertility and the Medical Treadmill

The Barriers of Infertility

*I*f open adoption is so promising, why doesn't every infertile couple—or single person for that matter—immediately leap onto this path to finding a child for their home? Part of the answer is that open adoption is new and many people have serious questions about the impact of the openness on their lives. But there is often another dimension to their hesitation: the demoralizing impact that their infertility has had on their sense of self-esteem, their self-respect, and their lives in general.

Ideally, people would discover at a young age that they were going to have trouble conceiving or giving birth to a healthy child. Then, when they were married and ready for a family, they would just check in at their local adoption center and soon they would have a baby. But that is not how it happens. Instead, most people consider adoption only after years of physical and emotional turmoil related to their inability to have a child on their own. Because of its intense emotional impact, infertility can affect a couple's chances for parenthood in two different ways. There is the obvious obstacle of the medical problem itself. But there is also the emotional impact. For many men and women, the barrage of testing and treatments for infertility is so depressing that they feel trapped on a virtual medical treadmill, unable to call a halt to treatments and begin pursuing adoption. For others, though they do turn to adoption, their experiences with infertility have been so demoralizing that they choose older, less hopeful forms of adoption rather than more promising, more open approaches to finding a child to parent.

Why is infertility so devastating? How do people get beyond this pain to start pursuing a family through open adoption?

The Strain of Infertility

*M*ost modern couples worry about unplanned pregnancies, not infertility. They exercise great care to avoid having a child before they are ready. Discovering that they are likely to have serious problems conceiving or giving birth usually comes as a shock. Were all those years of carefully using birth control just a mistake or a waste of time or both? The second shock comes when the couple realizes that a cure may not be easy, or even possible at all. Most people begin the requisite medical treatment—from medication to surgery—certain that it is only a matter of time before they, too, will become parents. After all, they reason, there are so many medical miracles these days: triple bypass heart surgery, the elimination of diseases like smallpox or polio. Besides, infertility does not seem that large a puzzle to solve.

They have met and overcome other barriers before; this will just be one more to handle. These men and women, after all, are part of the so-called baby boom generation, a generation more accustomed to success than failure. They have worked hard to make whatever changes are needed in their lives to reach their personal objectives. They get married, and if necessary, get divorced. Jobs or even careers are changed, if needed, to find the best type of work life. People move from city to city to find the right community environment. But then comes infertility, and for the first time, nothing seems to work, no matter how much effort they put into it. Years go by with no pregnancy. For many men and women, the struggle with infertility is the first time they have felt so hopeless about reaching their goals. Their difficulties having a baby can seem like a slow death, as the child of their dreams seems to dissolve in a haze of scheduled sex, medications, operations, and temperature charts.

Infertility is usually defined as the failure to become pregnant after a minimum of six months to one year, but a broader definition is more appropriate. For many people, the problem is conceiving a child. The problem may be with the man or the woman's reproductive system, or, most often, with both. Other couples manage to become pregnant only to go through the anguish of multiple miscarriages. There are women who may be physically able to become pregnant and give birth, but not without a serious health risk either to themselves or, genetically, to the child. Then there are couples in which one or both partners have become voluntarily sterile—usually during a previous marriage—and now both want to create a new family. For some women, age makes pregnancy unlikely or life-threatening. And finally, there are people, primarily women, who want to become parents despite their lack of a mate. Each of these problems is unique, but there is also a common thread: a profound sense of frustration about not being able to become a mother or father or the parents of another child.

I just assumed I would be a mother, so postponing parenting did not seem like a big deal. I could travel, find the right man and interesting work. When I had a child, I would be a mother and have a full life as well. I did find the right man and the right job but then, the shock. No matter what we did, we could not have a baby. At first, it seemed confusing, then almost funny—after all those years of birth control pills and diaphragms and condoms and all that worrying if my period was just a little late.

Then it was not funny anymore. I liked my job a lot but that could not be my whole life. How could I live never having been a mother? I just could not imagine that, and yet it was happening. It tore me apart and threatened to tear apart my marriage. All my friends were sympathetic but they all had kids already and just did not understand. Sometimes I would be with a group of my women friends and they would be complaining about their kids not being perfect and I wanted to scream out my pain. But they would never understand.

❖ At the time, my decision made sense. I had two children already and clearly did not want any more. So why not have a vasectomy? Now ten years later, I want to share parenting with my new wife. But nothing is working, despite two operations. Every single month, just when my wife is feeling most vulnerable—she gets that sharp reminder most people call a menstrual period. We call it the "Remember again, you are NOT pregnant" reminder. I keep feeling like I have cheated my wife out of parenthood. I can't imagine a worse thing to do to someone.

After seven years of my own personal infertility, I finally did have a child, biologically. But the bitter memories of infertility still linger. I can recall a time, ten years go, when I was asked to give a talk about infertility at a San Francisco

Bay Area conference on men's health. Before the talk, which happened to be on Father's Day, at least a dozen men asked me how old my child was. Each time somebody posed the question, I winced and explained that I did not have any children yet. I tried to explain that my wife and I had been trying unsuccessfully to get pregnant for years and years, but it became harder and harder to keep repeating my story. After several hours, I felt so desperate about not being a father that I did something I did not think I was capable of: I actually hid away in an unused room in the building. I came out only to give my little speech. Recently, I was watching a cute McDonald's commercial on TV. The father is driving his young daughter over to McDonald's only to be told that she does not want him to come in with her now that she is "older." For a minute, I felt a wave of pain as I thought to myself, "Will I ever be a father? Why can't *I* have a daughter?" It took me a while to remind myself that I was a father and that, in fact, my daughter was sitting right next to me. Those years of infertility have left their scars.

In the 1960s and 1970s, there was less pressure on infertile couples. During those decades, creating a career rather than becoming a parent was foremost in many people's minds. People's infertility was hardly noticed. Everyone just assumed the couple had decided not to have children yet. Today, with a mini-baby boom among thirty- to forty-year-olds, all that has changed. Couples trying to have their own child can find themselves regularly exposed to baby showers, birth announcements, and lengthy conversations about babies and children. Some infertile couples become so depressed they begin to wonder if they even deserve to be parents. Maybe they forfeited their right to be a mother or father because they waited too long? Maybe they are just not parent "material"?

❖ Almost all our friends were two-career people with no children. Then suddenly, they all started having children. Except us. Sure, I know it's a medical problem—

I have a medical background myself and I even understand all the terminology. But sometimes I find myself wondering if maybe it's not a medical problem at all; maybe I just do not deserve to be a mother.

The common nonmedical explanations for infertility reinforce this sense of personal failure. In some ways, we have not come far from the days when childless couples were labeled barren, cursed by God. Infertility is often correlated with sexually transmitted diseases or a Yuppie life-style of self-indulgence. Whatever the specific explanation, infertility is usually seen as the couple's own fault.

In reality, age and health problems may both be factors in the increase in infertility, but their roles are exaggerated. While a woman's fertility does decline as she gets older, a man's does not until late in life. Most men are about as fertile in their forties as they were in their twenties. So, if age itself were the main factor, then almost all the infertility would be female, not male. But that is not the case: anywhere from 30 to 50 percent of infertility is related to medical problems with the man. Clearly there are broader forces at play here than age, forces outside the control of individual couples. These include everything from the sterilizing effects of IUDs—originally touted as a great form of birth control—to a variety of chemicals and drugs that men and women encounter at work or in the environment. Interestingly, the three countries in the world that have serious infertility problems are the United States, Japan, and what was formerly West Germany. What these nations have in common is not widespread venereal disease, delayed childbearing, or two-career families but high levels of industrialization, stressful life-styles, and environmental and workplace hazards.

Couples trying to overcome their infertility often do so in terrible isolation. Their usual sources of encouragement and support may be compromised or limited by the nature of the infertility itself. Since most people decide to have a child in part because of the strength and stability of their marriage, their spouses should be an important source of support for them as they go through the infertility process. Yet the struggle for a biological child can have a devastating impact on a marriage. Couples may wonder if the fact that they cannot have a child shows that there is something wrong in their relationship. They may feel deprived of intimacy and connection in their sexuality since the focus is on sex for reproduction, rather than for caring and affection. They may blame their spouses for their infertility problems. Or, vice versa, they may blame themselves and feel guilty about inflicting childlessness on their partners. There are no statistics on how many divorces result, but the emotional strain of infertility may well be an important factor in many marital problems.

> ❖ We have had such a good marriage but all this infertility makes me wonder. If everything is really okay, then why can't we get pregnant? Maybe I am in the wrong marriage. Worse, maybe it's the other way around. Maybe I should let my husband go. Wouldn't it be fairer to let him remarry so he could have a child with someone else? I know how much he wants to be a father.

Many people are too embarrassed to talk about their infertility problems with their friends or family. They cut themselves off from that possible source of support and nurturing. I usually ask participants in my adoption seminars to talk about their infertility problems. For many of them, it is the first time they have talked to anyone outside of their marriage about these issues, though they may have been undergoing medical treatment for years. When people do tell their friends and relatives about their problems, the response is often more harmful than helpful. Most people find infertility mysterious, hopeless, and even threatening. All too often, they simply repeat the litany of well-meaning but hackneyed, frustrating, and humiliating advice that every infertile couple learns to dread: "Just relax," "Drink a glass of wine," "Take a vacation," or even sometimes, "I told you, you should have had kids a long time ago." Once again, each of these responses blames the couple for their own infertility. They are infertile because they are too tense, too overworked, or too concerned with their careers. Not only are these remarks not helpful, but they reinforce the negative impact infertility has probably already had on the couple's self-esteem.

❖ If one more person tells me to relax or take a vacation, I will scream. How can I do anything like that when I am in such pain about ever being a parent and when everybody is giving me so much advice? Besides, relaxing is not going to change the scarring on my tubes or my husband's low sperm count. All this advice does is make me feel worse and, believe me, I feel bad enough already.

Though infertility is not life-threatening, the medical treatments are unusually disruptive and invasive. Many of the tests and treatments—which can run into the thousands and sometimes tens of thousands of dollars—are not covered by health insurance. Reproductive systems are amazingly complex, and the science of infertility treatment is in its infancy. Even identifying the cause of the problem, much less finding a solution, can be a nightmare.

❖ "Okay," Ms. Jorgensen, my infertility specialist told me, "you and your husband need to have intercourse tomorrow morning before 8:00 A.M. Then be sure you are here by 9:30 A.M. sharp so we can do an exam to see if your husband's sperm and your cervical mucus are healthy enough." Sex on demand, that's terrific, and we even let the doctor tell us exactly what time to do it. And worst of all, sex not for pleasure at all but only for reproductive or testing purposes. After a while, all that counts is one goal (and one test)—male ejaculation. Pleasure or intimacy become irrelevant.

How often can you have that kind of sex before all sex—and even intimacy—becomes tainted?

Soon we get the results of that 9:30 A.M. test: nothing new. With the next test, I find out if I am allergic to my husband's sperm. It all does wonders for your self-esteem.

❖ Then there's the hamster test. They took my sperm and tried to impregnate a hamster egg. It didn't work, so it will not work for human beings either. The jokes are endless and pretty good at that, but somehow it does not feel funny.

❖ My favorite infertility treatment was Clomid, a powerful hormone that is supposed to induce the right cycle for my wife. It's the drug of choice these days. If you ask the doctor, they say there is a 2 to 5 percent chance of "emotional complications." But talk to any ten infertile couples using Clomid, and eight will tell you that it makes the woman feel depressed beyond reason and the husbands want to sue for divorce. And the effects are felt every single month.

Many infertility treatments such as in vitro fertilization (commonly referred to as IVF) are serious medical procedures requiring powerful medicines and complicated operations.[1] Years ago—since this procedure was expensive and rarely successful—it was prescribed only in desperate situations. Today, its use by infertile couples has become almost routine. The cost is typically about five thousand dollars per procedure. The procedure is rarely successful—only 10 to 15 percent of procedures result in pregnancy. Complications like miscarriages and tubal pregnancies are not uncommon. It is understandable how this process can leave couples in despair.

❖ Three attempts spread out over seven months. Shots every day, life with the side effects of Pergonal, battles with the insurance company to try and get them to absorb some of the cost (now over fifteen thousand dollars). Finally, on the third attempt at IVF, just when we were about to give up because we were so exhausted, financially and emotionally, it finally worked. She was pregnant! And then a few days later, she had a miscarriage. We felt a pain beyond pain. We had done everything, everything, everything, and nothing worked.

Infertility and the Medical Treadmill

*P*ursuing a medical solution for their infertility makes sense for most people. Medical treatments often do work: many of the people initially diagnosed as infertile are able to have a child biologically. But this is usually within the first year of medical intervention. If the treatments have not succeeded within a year or so, the chances of success fall dramatically. We would expect, then, that most people would try the medical path for a year, and then consider either adoption or just not having children. But that is not what happens. Some people do find it easy to switch from receiving medical treatment to pursuing parenthood through adoption: the medical treatment may seem too expensive or too invasive, or their medical problems may simply be untreatable. But these people are the exceptions. Most couples find it difficult to call medical intervention to a halt and, instead, find themselves trapped on a virtual medical treadmill. Why?

To begin with, there seems to be almost no end to the number of possible cures to attempt. Most normal medical problems have one or two possible courses of treatment; not infertility. If you have strep throat, for instance, you take one or another of the major antibiotics. If you have diabetes, there are various diet regimens to follow and insulin treatments to administer. And the treatments usually work. With infertility, though, there is an almost limitless number of possible solutions today. This has not always been the case. Ten years ago, when I directed an infertility clinic in San Francisco, there were only about six months' worth of possible treatments, including everything from baking soda to reduce the vaginal pH, to Clomid, to tubal surgery. If none of these approaches worked, the doctors gave up or went on to procedures that were considered shots in the dark, such as trying new, untested drugs or retrying a past treatment in the hope that this time it would work.

Today there are many new approaches to infertility. Some—like men avoiding hot baths or wearing looser underwear or even wearing cold compresses in their shorts to increase their sperm counts—sound like old-fashioned home remedies, but they are actually new. Then there are the high-technology approaches, from in vitro fertilization and a variety of new drugs to a multitude of new procedures often described by such intiials as GIFT, ZIFT, AIH, DI, GnRh, HCG, CVS. Almost all of these are difficult, time-consuming, and expensive productions but each has worked on somebody, somewhere, sometime. The medical profession deserves credit for having developed so many approaches to curing infertility. We can never adequately thank the doctors and researchers who make possible the joy of becoming a parent. Yet the very variety of possibilities makes deciding when to stop that much more difficult.

The medical terminology used in infertility treatment can itself add to a couple's feelings of being overwhelmed and unable to control the process. Many of the procedures, like a hysterosalpingogram, are tongue twisters. After a year of infertility treatments, most couples have learned so many new medical terms that they could practically qualify for a certificate as "Interns in Ob/GYN Infertility." Moreover, the medical terms, probably unintentionally, often imply that there is something morally, not just physically, wrong with the patient. For years, for instance, doctors referred to endometriosis, a chronic inflammation in or around a woman's tubes, as the "working woman's disease." Supposedly this problem did not occur among women who gave up their careers for motherhood and had babies in their early twenties. Although many doctors today have serious doubts about this connection, women with endometriosis are left feeling guilty that they chose to build their careers before having children. Or consider the process of chemically removing impurities in the man's sperm, usually done in connection with in vitro fertilization. The procedure helps ensure that the highest quality sperm is used to inseminate the eggs that have been removed from the woman's body. But the terminology—sperm washing—implies that the quite normal impurities in a man's sperm make it dirty. If a woman's cervix cannot hold the fetus, she is said to have an "incompetent" cervix. If she has started menopause earlier than is usual for most women, she is not described as being in early menopause, a reasonably neutral term, but as having premature menopause. None of these diagnoses leaves people feeling good about their bodies.

Even though the medical intervention in their lives can be so painful, many couples feel they have no choice but to continue pursuing medical treatment, no matter what the financial or emotional costs. A few years ago, a prominent infertility doctor told *USA Today* that his job would be easier if his patients did not get so emotional about becoming parents.[2] But that is just it. Many couples get to the point where life seems empty without a child. No matter what their career accomplishments or their financial successes, no matter how rich or famous they are, they feel their lives are at a dead end unless they can become parents. Halting medical treatment seems like giving up all hope.

The infertile couple's desperation may be fueled by the fear that any baby they have by an alternative method—adoption, surrogacy, or donor insemination—will never feel the same as the child they might have had biologically. For many wives, their ability or inability to bear a child is closely tied to their sense of identity as a woman. Conception, pregnancy, and childbirth seem so central to the definition of being female. The feelings of many husbands are similar. In spite of the changes in the definition of male roles in recent years, a man's ability to get his wife pregnant and have his own child still remains part of our society's test of manhood. For couples who have these common feelings, medical treatment seems the sole path to parenthood.

Years ago, political analysts discovered that revolutions are usually made, not by desperate people, but by people who see some glimmer of hope. Hopelessness makes people passive, not willing to take risks. Such desperation breeds passivity not only at the level of social movements, but at the personal, individual level as well. We might expect that the emotional and financial toll of infertility would make people rebel against seemingly ceaseless medical treatment. Unhappily, the feelings of hopelessness and helplessness associated with infertility treatment more often lead people to inertia.

Thankfully, though, people do not have to stay stuck on the medical treadmill. And thousands of people have stepped off. Couples (and single people) can find support by joining groups founded especially to assist people in coping with their infertility, such as Resolve, a nationwide infertility organization, or by going to adoption programs for help. For many people, the turning point comes when they finally realize that if they hold out for everything—the experience of pregnancy and childbirth and having a family—they may end up with nothing. They are ready to mourn the loss of pregnancy and childbirth, and to move on to the most important goal: the joy of being a mother or father. They realize that whether that baby comes biologically or through adoption is just not important.

❖ When we both realized that our infertility treatments had become like hoping for the pot of gold at the end of the rainbow, we knew it was time to move on.

❖ I was sitting in my doctor's waiting room when I suddenly realized something. I liked my doctor but what he wanted and what we wanted were different. He wanted to *cure* my infertility—and that's what doctors are there for, to cure things. But we did not want a cure, we wanted a *baby*. We called an adoption program the next day.

❖ For both of us, having our own child seemed terribly important. But then I started noticing that what made my friends so excited about being parents had little to do with biology. They were thrilled when the baby smiled at them for the first time or said its first word or called them mommy and daddy or showered them with that love that only a baby can give. At those amazing moments, the issue of where the baby came from seemed so totally and completely irrelevant that it was almost funny that I was worried about that. Sure, pregnancy and birth stuff—conception, sperm, eggs, fallopian tubes, Lamaze, and on and on—had been nice for them, and I was sorry I would miss that. But that was way behind them now as parents. That rarely entered their minds anymore. They were too busy with their love affairs with their babies. Biology—who cared anymore?

In fact, through adoption, women and men alike come to understand that parenting is not about conception or biological origins but about the profound relationship between a parent and a child.

❖ I met an old friend I had not seen for years. She was thrilled to find out that I had a child—now six years old. When she found out that my daughter, Meagan, was adopted, though, she asked me if I ever regretted that I could not have a baby on my own. I started to answer, "Yes, of course," when a surge of terror swept over me. I realized that if those infertility treatments had worked back then I would not have Meagan, I would have someone else. I felt almost faint. I adored Meagan. I could not

even imagine my life without her. I did not want any
other child but my child, Meagan.

Notes

1. After six to twelve months of testing without any success in
identifying the cause of the couple's infertility, many infertility spe-
cialists will recommend undergoing what has come to be called "in
vitro." This is a procedure in which a woman's eggs are fertilized
outside the woman's body and then placed directly into her uterus.
In preparation for this operation, the woman is given Pergonal, a
powerful medication that increases her production of eggs. Because
the drug has to be taken by injection a few times a day, often the
husband has to give the injection as an alternative to twice daily
visits to the doctor's office. Frequent blood checks are also required
because the medication used is so potent. During the initial operation, the doctor "harvests" the woman's eggs, which are then placed
with the man's sperm in a sterile dish. The man's sperm has also
been treated or "washed" by a special chemical and mechanical
treatment that removes any impurities. After the eggs have been
fertilized, the doctor carefully places one or more inside the woman's
body. Then the couple waits, hoping that one of the eggs becomes a
fetus.

2. *USA Today*, Thursday, September 26, 1985, page 9A.

4

Birthparent Stereotypes
and Realities

The Stereotypes of Birthmothers and Birthfathers

*P*art of people's hesitation about pursuing open adoption comes from their fears about birthparents. They have heard such terrible stories about these women, not to mention the men. Why on earth would they want any type of connection with these people? Wasn't closed adoption right to limit the rights of these irresponsible women and men? Why would anyone want to grant them so much power over the babies and the adopting parents? This initial hostility and suspicion are reflected in the questions most people ask about birthparents when they inquire about open adoption. "Do they use drugs, or have AIDS?" "Aren't many of these women out there just trying to get money from us and even willing to commit fraud to get it?" "How can I trust somebody who got pregnant so young?"

This negativity is hardly surprising. Our society's stereotypes about birthmothers and birthfathers are generally harsh and unforgiving. Birthmothers are seen as abandoning their children. Society sees them as some mixture of weak, poor, promiscuous, unhealthy, and uneducated, possibly they're even prostitutes, alcoholics, drug users, or AIDS carriers. All the above stereotypes—and even worse—apply to birthfathers. The birthmother is, at least, carrying the baby to term. The expectation of the birthfather is that he probably dropped out of sight the moment he found out his partner was pregnant.

In the last few years, a new stereotype of birthmothers has been added to this more traditional picture. "Wheeler-dealers" are what the media frequently call birthparents these days. In this view, the high demand for babies and the low supply of healthy infants puts once powerless birthmothers in the driver's seat. Birthmothers (and sometimes even the birthfathers) can ask for what they want and, if necessary, shop around until they find it. As a *Wall Street Journal* headline put it: "In Today's Adoptions, the Biological Parents Are Calling the Shots. With Demand Above Supply, Adoptive Parents Accede."[1] This stereotype may be an improvement over the view of birthparents as tramps, but the image is hardly favorable. The new picture may be more threatening to prospective adopting parents than the older view. Most adopting parents feel vulnerable enough already, without thinking that birthparents are slick manipulators.

The Realities About Birthparents

*I*f these stereotypes were true, people would have good reason to avoid open adoption. However, like many stereotypes, these, too, are inaccurate. Not all birthparents are saints. Some are mentally unbalanced or have used drugs or may even be outright frauds. Not only are these young people sad cases but a couple's involvement with them in an adoption can lead to pain and even tragedy. Yet these are the exception, not the rule. Most birthparents are thoughtful women and men, acting with considerable courage. Many people find it surprising that most birthparents are not teenagers: while birthparents in open adoption are anywhere from fourteen to forty years of age, the average birthparent is twenty to twenty-four years old. Moreover, several studies have shown that, compared to young women who choose abortion or single motherhood, birthmothers are above average in intelligence, have a higher sense of self-esteem, and, in the long run, are likely to be more successful in their lives.[2]

At first glance, this positive picture of birthparents may seem surprising. After all, part of what defines most is that they made a serious mistake. They got pregnant even though they were unprepared for the responsibilities of parenthood. But we need to see these young people's pregnancies in the context of contemporary social mores. Thirty years ago, few women got pregnant before they were married. That is not so today. No longer is a pregnant girl whisked off in secrecy and sent away to a hidden home for unwed mothers. Today, pregnancy has become almost a status symbol among young people. By the mid-1980s, nearly 10 percent of young women were becoming pregnant before the age of nineteen.[3] For young men, the trend is similar. Within that context, the fact of the birthparents' pregnancy is neither unusual nor shocking.

But even if not out of the ordinary, the birthparents' pregnancy may still have been a serious mistake. For some birthparents, their pregnancy was the result of a problem with their birth control methods. After all, few birth control methods are 100 percent reliable. Nevertheless, most of these young men and women are not prepared to be parents. They are far from financially secure, hardly surprising given their youth. Typically, if they are in a relationship it is not one stable enough to sustain a marriage. They are usually too young to try to handle, at the same time, the demands of both parenting and reaching their own social and educational goals.

What is striking about most birthparents, though, is not their mistake in getting pregnant, but their courage and foresight in handling that pregnancy. In choosing adoption, they make a conscious decision to control their lives rather than let the world roll over them—and their child. Unlike an overwhelming majority of pregnant young women (and their partners), they refuse to become parents before they are ready for that responsibility. These young people balk at becoming another sad statistic on the welfare roles. The mistake of becoming pregnant pales in the face of their courage in taking full responsibility for the consequences of their actions.

Another aspect of the stereotype is that birthmothers choose adoption in order to walk away from the responsibility of parenting. The opposite is usually the case. Consistently, birthparents—birthmothers in particular—decide on adoption because parenting is so important to them that they want to be parents at the right time and with the right partner. They do not feel emotionally or financially prepared to raise a child and rarely have a stable relationship with the child's birthfather. In the unusual case where the relationship is a good one, typically the birthmother is either not ready to make a permanent commitment—marry the birthfather—or they both agree that they are not ready to become parents together. Yet, while they may be deciding to have someone else raise their child, they are not throwing away parenthood. Choosing to have their child adopted is itself a *parenting* choice, a terribly difficult decision about what would be in the best interest of their child in the long run.

In fact, not only do these birthmothers have the courage to make the difficult decision for adoption, they choose the most challenging alternative, open adoption. In the long run, closed adoption can be damaging to a birthmother but, in the short run, it is far less complicated. She does not have to agonize over deciding who will have her baby, make any effort to develop a lifelong relationship with new people (the adopting parents) or have any responsibility to stay in touch with the adoptive family. All that closed adoption requires of her is to sign the correct legal papers. The agency takes care of everything else. They can literally walk away and hope they never have to look back.

But they do not want to walk away. For these birthparents, abandoning a child to a stranger, never to see him or her again, is unacceptable. So they turn to open adoption even if this approach requires so much more of them. With open adoption, the birthparent has the immense responsibility of selecting who will raise her baby, not temporarily, not even for one year or two, but forever. The birthparents open themselves up to building a relationship with strangers (the adopting parents). And their responsibility does not end once the baby is born. The birthparents have to find ways to keep in touch—even if only every year or two—with their child and the new adoptive family.

What is remarkable is that they choose this difficult route although they are feeling vulnerable about the pregnancy, about their relationship—or lack of relationship—with their partner, and about their general decision to choose adoption for their child. Despite their pain and even desperation, they choose open adoption. In fact, most not only seek out open adoption, but insist on it.

❖ When I saw the ad for an open adoption in a national paper, I knew that was what I wanted. When I called the open adoption place, they were very nice. But when I told Laura, their counselor, that I was due in only five or six days and was two thousand miles away, they said they did not think they could help. I shouldn't fly or travel with the baby due so soon, they explained. I appreciated that they were worried about me but I wanted an open adoption. Since there was none in my state, I was willing to go anywhere to find what I knew was right for myself and my baby. I arrived at their office just two days later and I got my open adoption. There was just no other way for me.

Finally, people often assume that most birthparents come from broken homes and are desperate not to have their child repeat their own sad lives. This is sometimes the case: many young people today are in family situations that are far from ideal. But more often the opposite is true. The birthmother and birthfather feel positive about their families and their parents. What they want is for their child to have a childhood more like their own than they can provide. And that means a mother and a father and a stable home. For this reason, birthparents are often drawn to prospective adopting parents who remind them of their own mothers and fathers.

Scams and Wheeler-dealers

What of the newest stereotype of birthparents as the wheeler-dealers of adoption? Or, even worse, the notion that many birthparents are not birthparents at all, but con artists trying to take advantage of people suffering from infertility?

The scam issue needs to be put to rest right away. Certainly anyone who tries to take advantage of the vulnerability of prospective adoptive parents should be condemned and, if at all possible, subject to the severest legal penalties. But these situations are rare. For instance, of the thousands of adoptions we have handled at the Independent Adoption Center, only a half dozen have turned out to be actual scams. Other open adoption programs have a similar record. Considering that, unfortunately, we live in a society where fraud is not uncommon, this is a low number. When scams do happen, invariably little or no counseling has been provided to any of the parties.

While a woman could pose as a potential birthmother, the deceit is not likely to survive her participation in a comprehensive counseling program. During the course of this type of intense counseling, any deceptions are likely to be spotted and revealed.

The image of a swaggering birthmother is simply not the reality of what most birthmothers are like. Few birthparents approach adoption feeling that way. If anything, they are the ones who feel nervous.

> ❖ It took me weeks to get up the courage to call about having my baby-to-be adopted. I must have started to dial the number and then hung up a dozen times without even finishing dialing. A few times, I even dialed the number and hung up after the first ring. When I finally called, I was in tears. I was confused. I felt ashamed that I had gotten pregnant. Most of all, I wanted the counselor to tell me that it was normal for me to feel so guilty about wanting to give up my child. I was sure they would think I was terribly selfish. Since I have red hair and freckles, I was even afraid they might not have a couple that would want to adopt my baby.

Health Issues in Open Adoption

One of the most common concerns of adopting parents is the health of the birthmother and the baby. Many people associate birthmothers with drugs, alcohol, poor health, and questionable genetic inheritance. All are concerned about adequate prenatal care.

There have indeed been cases in which governmental agencies remove babies from birthmothers because of drug use or a history of child abuse; adopting a baby in such a situation must be approached with great care. But most open adoptions are a matter of choice by the birthparents. Not only are most birthmothers as healthy as most pregnant women, but the very nature of the open adoption process tends to screen out birthmothers with high-risk mental, drug, or alcohol-related problems. Because abortion and single parenting are easier and more socially accepted, choosing adoption requires considerable maturity and fortitude. Such characteristics are not common among people who abuse drugs or alcohol or have unhealthy life-styles, physical or mental. Open adoption counselors are trained to identify serious drug abuse or mental problems, but few report that they find many birthmothers with these problems.

The free access to information characteristic of open adoption is especially important in regard to health issues. In closed adoption, health records are not available to either party, before or after the birth. Agencies feel that such medical records would provide too much revealing information. This is not an issue in open adoption. The birthparents sign a routine release of information and the adopting parents then have access to their complete medical histories. If, years later, new questions arise about the child's genetic or biological background, the initial medical information can easily be supplemented because of the adopting parents' ongoing contact with their child's birthparents.

Genetics and inheritance are another issue. A doctor can advise the adopting parents of any indications of serious genetic problems with either of the birthparents. An example would be a family history of illness known to have possible genetic connections, such as diabetes or heart disease. Where appropriate, testing for genetic problems such as Tay-Sachs or Sickle Cell Anemia can be done. If there are any indications of serious risk, the adopting couple has to decide whether to continue exploring a match with the particular birthmother and birthfather.

But many prospective adopting parents are also concerned about the inheritance of general intelligence or specific personality characteristics. Certainly with adoption, the children will not be inheriting their adoptive parents' genes. But biological parents cannot be sure that their children will be like them either. Today geneticists tell us that a variety of characteristics can be passed from one generation to the next: intelligence, athletic ability, musical talents, and resistance or susceptibility to medical or mental problems. But, although inheritance is important, scientists are nowhere near understanding the specific mechanics of how inheritance works. A man and woman who are both exceptionally athletic, for instance, may have their own biological child who inherits a distant relative's almost total lack of ability in sports. Most biological parents of two or three children find each child quite different in temperament and talents though they are all from the same genetic pool. In the end, neither biological parents nor adoptive parents can be sure that their children will be like them.

In that context, most adoptive parents are no better or worse off than biological parents in being able to ensure that their child will inherit the "right" characteristics. Even so, a thorough check of the birthparents' genetic background is important. If problems come to light, they need to be carefully considered. But by adopting someone else's child, the adoptive parents are generally giving up what is only a mythical control of their child's inheritance and simply adding a few more variables to the mixture.

But Can They Choose the Right People to Be the Parents of Their Child?

Open adoption acknowledges the right of birthparents to decide who will raise their children. But many people wonder if these young people can be trusted to make such important decisions. Won't they pick out people with the characteristics that most teenagers value the most: youth, glamour, thinness, fame, and fortune? In fact, birthparents do not choose on the basis of age, glamour, or weight; rather, they look for people who they think will make the best parents. They are concerned most about a family's stability and values, and simply whether they seem like nice people. Some birthmothers are drawn to younger people because they imagine they would make more energetic parents. But, contrary to most people's expectations, more often birthparents are less concerned about age than whether the new parents are settled in their careers, lives, marriages, and homes; frequently people in their thirties and forties or even older are preferred. Rarely is wealth or glamour any type of criterion. In fact, some birthparents are reluctant to choose a rich or famous couple for fear that their child will be spoiled or kidnapped or too much in the limelight.

The criteria used by most birthparents are consistently more openminded and thoughtful than those imposed by traditional agencies with all their restrictions based on age, health, and family size.

❖ We had six adopted children and wanted a seventh. The regular agencies just turned us down flat, so we went the open route. But even they seemed worried that we had little chance since we already had so many kids. They worried that all those other couples with no children would get picked first. But my wife and I knew in our hearts that everything would be fine. Sure enough, within four months, a birthmother chose us. She came from a happy family of eight kids and the last thing she wanted was for her child to be an only child or in a small family. Once she saw the picture of my wife and me and our six kids, she did not even bother to read any other letters. She knew she had found what she wanted.

❖ My wife is profoundly deaf and everyone told us that we would simply not be the choice of any birthmother because of her handicap. But we decided to give it a try anyway. I "signed" all the educational sessions for my wife so she would know everything that was going on. In only a few months, a birthmother picked us to adopt her soon-to-be twin boys. It turned out that her own mother had a serious hearing problem and she knew what that was like and knew that it made little difference. But it was even better than that. Throughout the pregnancy, we worried about the birthfather. He was in the service and we could not get hold of him. What if he showed up at the last minute and was a problem? He did show up at the last minute but not only was he supportive, but it turned out he knew how to use sign language.

Birthfathers

Generally, I have referred to birthparents as if birthmothers and birthfathers were equally involved in open adoptions. In reality, the primary person in most adoptions is the birthmother, not the birthfather. I would like to say that the stereotypes of birthfathers are as wrong as the stereotypes of birthmothers. But I cannot. Many birthfathers do fit the old stereotype: they are—as some birthmothers put it—"history" the moment they find out their partners are pregnant. After all, the man can disappear and pretend nothing ever happened. The birthmother does not have that choice. Yet more and more birthfathers choose to be a genuine part of the open adoption process. In as many as one fourth of open adoptions today, the birthfather takes an active role.

This change probably reflects broader developments in our society about the role of fathers. In recent years, fatherhood has evolved into more than just being the family breadwinner. For instance, some men are even demanding (and getting) paternity leave. Not surprisingly, then, birthfathers are starting to play an ever-increasing role in open adoption. They, too, want to make the best parenting choice for their child.

❖ Kelsey [the birthmother] and I [the birthfather] were barely making it, just the two of us. We were not putting away any savings or anything. I was just out of high school and had no other formal education. We wanted to make sure that the baby had a good family and that they had good values and a good foundation. We were sad to see her go but I was glad that she had a family. She looks a lot like Kelsey. We are going to go on and do the things with our lives that we feel are right. We hope to make something of ourselves.

❖ At first, I [the birthfather] was angry but then I realized I could have some say too. It was my baby after all, even if we were not going to stay together. And that's all I wanted, to be some part of the adoption.

❖ Because of his cultural background—he was Asian— the birthfather seemed to be very resistant to our adopting his child. We tried to be patient and the counselor helped a great deal. He seemed okay after a while, but when the baby was born, he got very upset and refused to sign the papers and even went to a lawyer to start legal action. The counselor spent hours and hours with him, but he still seemed to be adamantly opposed to the adoption and unwilling ever to sign the papers. Finally, he agreed to meet with us and the counselor. We really did understand his feelings, but we were terribly worried and expected the session to be bitter. When we all sat down, he asked if he could say something. He told us that he had been thinking about everything and, as an act of good faith, had gone that same morning and signed all the legal papers needed for the adoption so we could all talk without that hanging over us.

Some birthfathers participate in individual counseling and birthparent support groups. They share in choosing the adoptive parents and are present at the birth. With their participation, the adoption process is invariably smoother and a more positive experience for everyone. Legal issues are more easily resolved, the birthmother has the birthfather's support for her decision, and the child has information and access to his or her biological father as well as biological mother.

Birthparent Stories

There are no "typical" birthparents or birthgrandparents, the parents of the birthmother or birthfather. A few do fit the worst stereotypes: they are plagued by mental illness or drug use or they are simply involved in some kind of scam. But most are exceptional young people trying their best to cope with difficult situations. Let me relate the stories of two birthparents that are representative. These were written by a birthmother herself in the first case, and by a birthgrandparent in the second case.[4]

Terri's Story

When I was seventeen years old I became a statistic. I was an unwed, pregnant teenager. I wasn't sure what to do. I wasn't even aware of my choices. I kept my baby and began the life of an unwed teenage parent.

It was very hard to be a parent so young. I was just learning how to take care of myself; I didn't have the skills to take care of another human being.

I worked very hard to be a good mother to my daughter. I started college and I took child development courses. I spent most of my free time with my daughter—talking, playing, learning, and growing. We were a team.

Well, you can't begin to imagine the feelings that went through me when I found I was pregnant again. And here my daughter was just two and a half years old. How could I possibly take care of another baby by myself? My relationship with the new baby's father was not good and I didn't foresee it getting any better. I was scared, angry, and ashamed. How could I let this happen to me again? What kind of girl did that make me? I had nothing to offer. If love was enough it would have been fine. It takes more than love and I knew that already. I decided I'd have an abortion.

This was a tough decision for me since I believe children are a gift from God. I just couldn't see any other solution. I called around to find out the cost of an abortion and the procedure involved. There was a small walk-in clinic in my neighborhood; a friend gave me the money and I was all set. I'd do it tomorrow.

Tomorrow came. A week of tomorrows came, and when I was six months along I went to the doctor and he did an ultrasound. All I could see on the screen was a small black circle. Then, in the center of that circle I could see something move, a heartbeat. Tears poured from my eyes as I watched my baby's heart beat. I left the doctor's office that day knowing I'd give birth.

I decided on adoption. I was sure that this baby could bring happiness to a couple. I was sure that there was a couple who could give my baby everything I wished I could. But how could I find them? Whom should I call? I called the United Way thinking that they'd know where to start. That first call was so hard. They referred me to several adoption agencies. I wrote down the numbers and tucked them away. I had to be sure what I wanted.

I wanted to meet the people who adopted my baby. I didn't want to just hand him over to someone I didn't know, say good-bye, and never see him again. I wanted the couple to

live in a different state. I did not want to look at babies at
the mall and wonder which one was mine.

I wanted them to be young and I wanted them to have
strong spirituality. Several weeks passed and finally I began
to make the phone calls. There was phone call after phone
call, agency after agency, worker after worker, and I didn't
feel right about it. None of the agencies would let me meet
the couple and none of them had couples from out of state.
It disturbed me that the agencies told me to come on in anyway and we could work something out. I didn't want to work
something out. I knew what I wanted and that was it. It was
my baby, not some automobile we could make a deal on. I
couldn't go through with it unless I felt okay with what was
happening. And I didn't feel okay with the agencies I called.

A friend told me about a classified column in *USA Today*
called "Adoption." This was exactly what I was looking for.
It was ads from couples all over the country who wanted to
adopt. I found an ad that said all the choices were mine. I
clipped this ad and called the number right away.

This number was for an open adoption center in California.
I spoke with the birthmom intake worker, Cara. For the first
time since this whole thing began I broke down and cried.
Cara was so sweet and loving. I knew her main concern was
me; her main concern was that I was okay with what was
happening.

She sent me a packet of information that included letters
from couples who wanted to adopt. This was exactly what I
wanted. Each letter had a photograph attached. I could look
at their faces. I could read, in their own words, about their
lives and how much they wanted a baby.

I met several couples. This really helped me because when
I finally met the right couple, I knew it was right. I ended up
living with them for the rest of my pregnancy. We developed
a love that goes deeper than any I have ever known. We plan
to continue contact through phone calls, letters, and visits.
Without open adoption I don't know what I would have done.

I was able to make my own choices and because of this I have a peace in my heart I thought I'd never know.

Karen and Mary's Story[5]

What does a mother do when she discovers her seventeen-year-old daughter is expecting a baby? After the initial shock and despair, I knew there was only one course of action. I had to gather my daughter into my arms, to assure her that an unintended pregnancy was not the end of the world, to pledge my support and love in helping her figure out what to do next.

Karen had decided that neither abortion nor marriage was an option. In fact, the baby's father had "bailed out" to the point that he denied paternity. Karen was left with only two choices.

I resisted the impulse to "make it all better." The obvious solution, which to my mind was no solution at all, was to invite my daughter to raise her children at home. In my mind's eye I could see her a few months down the road beginning to chafe under the yoke of motherhood. She would resent having a baby who kept her tied to a bassinet while her friends were out climbing mountains. My offers to help would be genuine but in time, might I not begin to harbor a certain resentment? The youngest of my four children was fourteen. I had my own mountains to climb.

The one remaining option was adoption. I confess that my understanding of modern adoption procedures was nil. Like 90 percent of the population, I thought the word adoption was synonymous with red tape, secrecy, and the severing of ties between a mother and her baby.

Karen was willing to explore the possibility of relinquishing her child. Somewhere she found the courage to admit that she had neither the financial, educational, nor emotional resources to provide the kind of life her child deserved. But she also knew that she could not simply give her baby away to strangers and never see it again. My daughter was at her lowest ebb when she contacted an open adoption center and first heard about this type of adoption. The procedures, she learned, would be open and honest, not shrouded in shame and secrecy. She would choose the adopting couple and remain in contact with them and her baby. "In an open adoption," her counselor explained, "there are no strangers, only friends."

My enthusiasm matched Karen's. I devoured every available piece of literature on open adoption. My husband and I went for counseling at the center. Yet, unconsciously, I kept my emotions under wraps. I did not allow myself the grandma's prerogative to coo and cluck and picture new branches on the family tree. When the counselor tried to explain that, like my daughter, I, too, would go through a grieving process after the birth, I smugly dismissed the notion; this baby was not my grandchild; it was just a baby my daughter was going to have. Looking back I realize that I was insulating myself. What if the adopting couple's definition of open was different from my own? What if I counted on doors being thrown wide open only to discover that their preference was to open them just a crack?

Today Karen, her immediate family, and the adopting couple enjoy a loving relationship in which there are no barriers. We look upon ourselves as an extended family, sharing birthdays and holidays and above all a mutual love for a very special little girl. Baby Livia has two other grandmothers and I hope I have assured them that they need not fear me, the birth grandmother, invading their territory, demanding equal time and attention. If my only role is to sit back and enjoy, I am content. What will baby Livia think when she is old enough to understand that she has three grandmothers while other kids have only two? The three of us agree that Livia is lucky. How can an extra measure of grandmotherly love do anything but enrich her life?

Notes

1. *Wall Street Journal*, October 14, 1989, page 1.
2. Steven D. McLaughlin, et al, "The Consequences of the Adoption Decision," Final Report to the Office of Adolescent Pregnancy Programs, Battelle Human Affairs Research Centers, Seattle Washington, April, 1987. Unfortunately, there are no equivalent studies of birthfathers.
3. Alan Gutmacher Institute, *News*, March 1985.
4. These two stories were originally published in the Independent Adoption Center's special *Birthparent Directory*, made available to women and men considering having their child adopted. The pamphlet provides prospective birthparents with more details about open adoption from women and men their own age who have personally been through the process. The directory includes phone numbers so that the birthparents who wrote the stories can act as volunteer peer counselors by phone.
5. For the full story of Mary Stephenson's experience, see her book, *My Child Is a Mother* (San Antonio: Corona Publishing Co., 1991). Since Mary and Karen's story has already appeared in print, I am using their real names here.

5

The Surprising Bond Between
Adopting Parents and Birthparents

*E*ven if the stereotypes about birthparents are inaccurate, that is not enough to allay most people's concerns about birthparents. With closed adoption, the adopting parents need pay no attention to the birthparents. In fact, they are not allowed contact even if they desire it. With the advent of open adoption, the adopting parents are dependent on the birthparents going through with the adoption. They need to meet and get to know them and even earn their approval. And the connections with the birthparents may last a lifetime.

Considering the roller coaster ride of infertility, many adopting parents are reluctant to bring any new people into their lives, especially anyone they expect to be different from themselves. After so many years of trying to have a child, adopting parents may feel little sympathy toward, and little bond with, someone who became pregnant easily—maybe too easily. It does not help, either, that most adopting parents are fifteen to twenty years older than the birthparents and have different tastes in music, clothes, and general life-style.

There are other reasons why adopting parents may feel uneasy. The relationship between adopting parents and birthparents appears one sided: the birthparents seem to have all the power. They choose who gets the baby, they frequently dictate the terms of that gift, and, worst of all, they can change their minds.

> ❖ I felt bad enough about turning forty as it was. The fact that I still had no children made me feel a thousand times worse. When I saw pictures of some of these birthmothers, they all looked so young and healthy. There they were pregnant with just the baby I wanted and deserved. I knew I shouldn't, but I felt angry with all of them.

In some cases, the worst does happen. The birthparents act distant, even unfriendly, and are manipulative and demanding. Sometimes these difficulties characterize only the beginning of the relationship; other times, they span the entire length of the connection. In these situations, extensive and long-term counseling support is vital and the adoptive parents have to have considerable patience for the adoption to succeed. Needless to say, many of these adoptions do not work out. In other situations, although the relationship of the adoptive parents to the birthparents surprises everyone with its closeness and caring, the adoption does not succeed because the birthmother changes her mind after the child is born. The sense of loss and grief can be excruciating.

> ❖ Because of our age and because of our circumstances, we decided that adoption was the only way we were going to get a baby. So we contacted an open adoption center that had a complete counseling program.
> Our "match meeting" was a mutual interview. We

met the father and mother both. We fell in love with them, it was love at first sight. The counselors did warn us that the adoption was a major risk because they were, after all, a couple and seemed committed to each other. And they were both living with her parents. Marla was twenty-one and he was nineteen. She was eight months pregnant. But we decided to take our chances.

We were both at work when we got the call to come to the hospital. They were close to where we were and we got to the hospital in plenty of time. Bob [the adopting father] held her hand and the birthfather held her other hand. It was a little baby boy. He was born Friday about midnight and we took him home Saturday about noon. The hardest thing in this whole process was taking him away from his mom. Marla carried him out of the hospital. They wheeled her out in the wheelchair and, when we were all out there, she just handed him to us. She was becoming hysterical though she hadn't really shown much emotion until that point.

We were all very comfortable with the agreement for all of us to stay in contact. We really cared about them so that seemed natural. Friday, at noon, the counselor from the adoption center called. We had already heard several things during the week that made us worried. The birthparents hadn't come in for their usual counseling and the counselor was very concerned. This time, the counselor told me they had changed their minds and wanted the baby returned.

Of course I was hysterical. I called Bob at work and he came home. We cried most of the night and the next day. We called the birthparents at home and said, "You can come pick him up tonight. We know you've changed your minds. We'd like for you to come by as soon as possible." Marla said very little. Bob said some; he was kind of the spokesperson. They said that they were extremely sorry. They were in tears.

They didn't come that night but the next. They said that they were sorry they had hurt us so badly. By that time we had said our good-bye to our baby and had come to grips with the loss ourselves. Also we knew that this baby was going to be taken care of. They loved this baby so much and that's why they felt they'd made such a big mistake.

Sometimes these experiences are so devastating that the adoptive parents either turn to closed adoption or choose not to adopt at all. More often, they choose to try again.

❖ Our loss did not sour us on an open adoption. We understood the birthparents, even if we were so deeply hurt. In fact, we still hear from them occasionally.

We went right back to trying to adopt. We submitted our letter on our wedding anniversary, November 8. We were chosen a few months later and now are the parents of an amazing one-year-old little boy.

❖ Even after the ordeal of losing our child, I was still sure that open adoption was the path I wanted to continue pursuing. Even with the pain we experienced, the relationship we established with our birthmother was beautiful. I could not imagine adopting a child any other way. It was open adoption or not adopting.

Fortunately, the reality of most open adoptions is strikingly different from the experiences just described. Across the country, for instance, fewer than 5 to 10 percent of open adoptions fail in this way. Moreover—much to many people's surprise—extraordinarily strong bonds typically develop quickly and easily between the adopting parents and birthparents. The adopting parents not only come to accept the birthparents but find they care deeply about them. We often joke that we can barely keep adopting couples from adopting the birthparents as well as their babies. The adoptions go smoothly and the adoptive parents have the joy of a new baby.

And the relationship that seemed so scary initially becomes the critical factor that makes open adoptions succeed and allows the adoptive families to flower in a way unheard of with closed adoption.

The First Meetings Start the Bonding Process

*T*he bonding process begins with the first encounters between adoptive parents and birthparents. These "match meetings" bring the adopting parents and birthparents together to talk, face to face, for anywhere from one to three hours. For a good part of this initial meeting, a skilled counselor is present to facilitate the process, but part of the time the adopting parents and birthparents are left alone to talk.

Most people are nervous about these meetings. They expect the worst. They assume that they will be grilled mercilessly and then rejected. Some think the birthparents will swagger in, give them that knowing look that implies "I have something you want and I know it," and proceed to ask a series of questions that will make the interrogations of the Spanish Inquisition look tame by comparison. This nightmare fantasy concludes with the birthparents suddenly getting up and saying as they leave, "I certainly would not let *you* have my baby."

What comes as a surprise to adopting parents is that the birthparents feel just as threatened. They may have the same type of Spanish Inquisition fantasy, but they assume the interrogation will be directed against *them* by a self-centered, self-assured, and mature couple. The birthmothers, in particular, feel defensive. Because of the association in the past between adoption and illegitimacy, the minute they are introduced, many birthmothers announce immediately that they come from a good family, get good grades, and are not one of "those" girls. Their nightmare is that the prospective adopting parents will suddenly get up and say as they leave, "We certainly would not adopt a baby of *yours!*"

But none of these nightmares comes true. As the match meeting progresses—and the counselor guides everyone through the introductions—all parties soon realize that they are equally nervous and feel equally vulnerable. Each party asks and answers a lot of questions. Some of them are general: "What are your hobbies and main interests?" or "What are your plans for the future?" Many of the questions are specific to the situation. Birthmothers are commonly asked questions like these: "Why didn't you have an abortion?" "What about the birthfather and your relationship to him?" "What is your family's involvement in the adoption?" "What type of pre-natal care have you had?" "Why are you considering having your baby adopted?" The questions to the adopting parents run along these lines: "Why haven't you been able to have your own child?" "What has it been like to want a child so badly?" "Will the rest of your family accept an adopted child?" "Do you think you can love an adopted child as much as a biological child?" "What future plans do you have for yourself and the child?" Often people are shy about interrogating each other, so many of the questions are asked by the counselor. The depth at which people talk during these meetings is astonishing and the candor is equal on both sides. During this initial meeting, rarely does anyone feel one-up or one-down. Almost always, there is an honest exchange of information and often at a surprising level of intensity for people who have just met each other for the first time.

❖ My pregnancy had been the result of what is called date-rape these days: forced intercourse with somebody I knew. I told the counselor about it but I knew I would also have to tell the adopting couple, Tom and Martha. But I was not sure if I could.

We were all pretty nervous at the match meeting, but soon we all started to relax and to get to know each other.

Finally, I said, "There is something else I have to tell you. I do love this baby but the way it started out was terrible, horrible. Our sex together was not my idea. I was forced, attacked. It was awful." I started to cry.

Tom became teary but Martha began sobbing and sobbing. Finally, she turned to me and said, "I have never told anybody this, nobody, not my parents, not Tom, no one. And I have been sure I never would. I have kept this secret for so long that sometimes I almost forgot it ever happened. But not really. When I was sixteen, I was raped, too, and it was just like you said."

A moment passed, then Martha got up and came over to me. We held on to each other for a long time.

Of course, not all first meetings are this dramatic or the intimacy so immediate and intense. Yet most people new to open adoption are amazed at how different are the actual birthparents from what they imagined. Instead of the brash and desperate people they expect, they encounter quiet, decent, and thoughtful young adults. Perhaps adopting couples find these first meetings especially touching just because their expectations are so negative. Whatever the reason, the experience is usually "a 180-degree turnaround" in feelings about birthparents, as one adoptive mother explained to me. Or, as another adoptive mother said, "I went in hating her [the birthmother]. I came out wishing she were my daughter."

❖ The first time we talked it was like we were really good friends. Like we knew her. Everything connected. I talked to her several times during that first week. It was like we had known each other forever.

❖ You hear this from so many adoptive parents but it was true for us. Our birthmother walked in. She sat down. We looked into each other's eyes and that was it. She could look into our eyes and know that we were going to be really good for her son. We could look into her eyes and know that she was telling the truth, that she hadn't been doing drugs and all these things. It was that two-second exchange that did it.

❖ When we met Shelly, I was just blown away by her maturity and her warmth and the way that she had come to her decision. I felt at the time that there was no way I could deny her the right to see the child. As it turns out, I wouldn't deny *us* the right to be with Shelly either; she has been so good for us.

For many adopting parents and birthparents, these initial contacts are anxious moments but are often remembered with fondness.

❖ We met our birthmother for the first time two years ago today. It is with a lot of pleasure and joy that Jon and I remember that meeting. We had had several false starts already and just weren't sure what was going to happen. We had heard that you would "know" when a match was right but didn't quite believe it. But we did know the instant we met Kathy, before any of us said a word. She has said she felt the same way.

❖ When we went to meet our birthmother at the airport, I was really nervous about meeting her and what she would think about us. Then this friend of mine who adopted a baby said, "Remember, she's more nervous than you guys." Once I thought about that I said, "Yeah, that's true." But I still sat at the airport scared. I was afraid she wasn't going to show up.

But she was there! When she walked off the plane, though we had never met her or even seen a picture of her, we knew exactly who she was. We just connected. She said she could see us when the plane came in. I just looked and knew it was her.

And something else, too. When we introduced our-selves to her, we were so excited and we showed it. Later she told us how great that was for her. It was the first time anybody was excited about her being pregnant. Her parents wanted her to have an abortion. No one around her cared or wanted her to be pregnant. And here we were, so excited. Somebody actually cared!

Does this mean that every match works out? Obviously not. In some cases, the adopting parents and birthparents are not appropriate for each other. This type of mismatching probably occurs in about 10 percent of matches. They may have different expectations about how the child is to be raised, or there may be aspects of each other's lives and personalities that make them uncomfortable. Sometimes there are life-style differences, particularly around the issue of privacy. One or both members of the adopting couple may come from close families used to active, frequent, and intense contact. If they are matched with a birthmother with a more private, retiring life-style, this can be a problem. And the opposite can be the case as well: a more introspective adopting couple may clash with an outgoing birthmother. In certain situations, the birthparents feel that the couple (or single person) is different from what they expected and are no longer their choice to be the new parents. The same can be true for the prospective adopting parents in regard to the birthparents. In fact, contrary to many adopting couples' fears, in most open adoption programs, prospective adopting parents are much more likely to reject the birthparents than the other way around. If the match does not succeed for any of these reasons, everyone is, of course, disappointed. Yet birthparents and adopting parents alike have the chance to find this out for themselves by meeting and talking. As a result, they can go their separate ways in peace.

A good match does not always guarantee a successful adoption. Some adoptions are riskier than others. Although unusual, the most serious problems occur with those birthparents who have used drugs or have a history of mental illness or emotional problems. Other situations are risky as well. Some birthmothers refuse all counseling. Teenage birthmothers in particular tend to be wary of counseling, afraid that they will be manipulated or patronized. That can be a problem, since extensive counseling is usually so crucial in open adoptions. Outside influences are also critical. The support of close friends and family (particularly if the birthmother is still living with her parents) is important, since there is little support in society in general for choosing adoption.

An important factor is whether the birthmother or birthfather has some sort of plan for the future, even a vague one. If they are looking forward to going to school, entering a training program, or following a certain career path, they can see more clearly how parenthood makes little sense for them or their child. If, in contrast, they have few plans or hopes for the future, keeping the child and becoming a parent can all too easily be a way to fill that void.

There are also more mundane factors. An unusually young (under sixteen years old) or immature birthmother can have serious problems handling a decision of this magnitude. Birthmothers who choose adoption very late in their pregnancy (in the last six weeks or even later, for instance) may not have time to build strong enough bonds with the adopting parents and the adoption counselor. And these connections are so important for helping the birthparents through the pain and grief of their adoption choice.

Legal complications can also present a problem. Some states have unusually complicated regulations regarding private adoptions. A birthfather who is unknown, uninvolved, or hostile can complicate the legal proceedings. If the child has significant American Indian heritage, the legal complications can be almost overwhelming.

From Match to Birth: The Critical Connections Develop

*F*rom the match to the birth of the child may take six or seven months—or it may take no time at all, if the baby has already been born when the adoptive parents are chosen. In most open adoptions, though, there is typically a period of two to three months between match and birth. For a relationship of this intensity that can be a long and difficult time. Up to 10 percent of adoptions fall through during these weeks or months, more often than not because the adopting parents decide that the adoption is simply too risky. Nevertheless, most adopting parents find building a caring and solid relationship with the birthparents relatively easy. And that connection pays off! More than any statistic, more than anything anyone else tells them, it is the closeness of their relationship with the birthparents that most reassures them that their adoption is going to succeed.

The relationship begins with a form of mutual validation that is part of almost every open adoption. The adopting parents have been selected, not by an agency or lawyer or doctor, but by the birthparents themselves, often from among many other qualified and hopeful couples. Can there be a greater compliment than being chosen to parent someone's child?

To my birthson:
I have chosen Mark and Eleanor to be your parents. I have been with them for two months now. We have been together every day. I think they are very loving, understanding, giving, sincere people.
I'm not giving you up, Jason. *I'm not giving you to them. I've giving them to you.* I love them, Jason.

The validation is equally powerful from the birthparents' point of view. The adopting parents certainly must care about the birthparents a great deal. After all, they have agreed to raise this child as their own.

Yet people are still afraid that differences in ages and life-styles will be major problems. What they usually find, though, is the opposite. The youth of most of the birthparents turns out to be a positive, not a negative factor. For adopting parents, the adoption process offers an unusual opportunity to know members of another generation. In many ways, we are an age-stratified society. Some people have friends of all different ages, older and younger than themselves. But most people's primary friendships are with people close to their own age and only infrequently with people much younger than themselves. For adopting parents, the relationship with the typically young birthparents is often a rewarding experience for the very reason of their youth.

> ❖ It seemed that every time I turned on the TV, there was another teenager who was either a member of a gang or on drugs. I did not feel very hopeful for the future. Then I met the birthparents of my child-to-be. If they are representative of even a small part of that generation, we have nothing at all to worry about.

More important, adopting parents and birthparents find that their differences in age are less important than the many things they have in common. Perhaps they do not share the same favorite rock bands or movie stars or ideas about how best to spend an evening. But what they do share is more important: ways of looking at life, values, and, most crucial, a mutual understanding and respect for each other. These similarities are not accidental. Most birthparents choose a specific adopting couple because they have a set of values similar to their own. When asked what that means, most birthparents cannot be specific. It seems to be a feeling of kinship and connection. Often, they select people from a background similar to their own. This is not a matter of choosing someone from the same geographical area or someone with the same complexion or hair color. The semblances are more complex. For instance, most birthparents choose people from the same social class as their families. Although they do not always articulate their choice in that way, many birthparents make comments such as, "They seemed like people I would feel comfortable with." Often the attraction of a particular couple is subtle.

> ❖ When I looked through all the letters from people who wanted to adopt—about 120 of them—I chose the Jacksons right away. We all got along from the minute we met. When we realized that we were all born in Missouri, I was not surprised. Our counselor was, though. She asked me if I knew they were from Missouri when I picked them. I said, "Sure." She said, "How could you know that? It doesn't say anything about where they were born in their letter." "We Missourians just know these things," I replied.

Yet the feeling is no less strong for its subjectivity. Many of the important relationships we have in our lives are based on this same subjective sense of common values. For instance, when asked, most people can give some concrete explanation of why they married their spouse. They might mention age, intelligence, interests, or background. But, in truth, the decision was more subjective than objective. Most likely, they shared feelings about life, religion, families, beauty, and cultural issues. The connections between birthparents and adopting parents have the same quality of both subjectivity and depth.

The increasingly close bond between adopting parents and birthparents is the result not only of similar interests but also of the intense experience of sharing the birthmother's pregnancy with her. How close they are during that time varies a great deal, depending on how near each other they live and how soon the baby is due. Most adopting parents first meet their birthmother when she is in her sixth or seventh month. They may talk or visit with each other daily, weekly, or monthly. Most adopting parents, though—especially the adopting mothers—go with the birthmothers to the doctor, hear the baby's heartbeat through the doctor's stethoscope, look at the sonograms, and talk about how the pregnancy is progressing. They watch as the baby grows inside the birthmother and often get a chance to see—and feel—the baby kick. Although the adopting parents are experiencing the pregnancy vicariously, the feelings are still powerful. And in a way, the experience is not merely vicarious for the adopting parents, since this baby will soon be theirs.

> ❖ Simone had an amnio test done since she was over thirty-five. We went with her to the doctor for the results of the test. The doctor reported that everything was fine healthwise, and then asked Simone, "Do you want to know the sex of the baby?" With real pride and her particularly nice smile, Simone replied, "You have to ask the parents," pointing right at us. We just glowed. Then we said we did not want to know the sex. The doctor said fine, he would respect the wishes of the baby's parents.

A sense of mutual respect for each other's different pain and trials usually develops in these months before the birth. As they get to know the adopting parents better, birthmothers start to empathize with the pain the adopting parents have endured through their typically long search to find a way to become a mother and a father. For their part, adopting parents begin to understand how difficult was the birthparents' choice of adoption. As they become more familiar with the day-to-day lives of their birthparents, the adopting parents can see the pressure that is frequently put on the birthmother to decide *against* adoption. The pressure comes from peers, perhaps from the birthfather, from her family, or even from people in authority who are hostile toward adoption. And yet the birthmother (and perhaps birthfather) persist. It is hard not to be impressed by this fortitude and determination. Soon, they realize that the birthparents' vulnerability is often as great as their own, just not as apparent. Many birthparents are afraid that it will be the adopting parents who will change their minds. At the last minute, they will refuse to accept their baby. The birthparents are afraid that the adoptive parents will, literally, come to the hospital and say something like, "The baby is okay, but not quite as cute as we hoped. So good-bye."

> ❖ I called our adoption counselor in a state of panic. My baby had been born just a short while earlier and the adopting couple was on their way to see her. The birth had been fine, but the labor had been so short that Dennis and Patti had not been able to get there to see the child born. But that was not the problem. What I was worried about was that, though I have blond hair (true blond) and blue eyes, the baby had brown hair and brown eyes. Would Dennis and Patti be so disappointed about this that they would change their minds and not adopt my baby? The counselors reassured me that the couple would not even think twice about the baby's hair or eye color. That was just not important. Was I relieved.

The birthparents' risks are long-term as well as short-term. They are giving up their own child, forever. They take the chance that they will spend the rest of their lives regretting their decision and not being able to change it. Even in an open adoption, many birthparents worry that the adopting parents will not tell their child the truth about the adoption. Perhaps they will not even tell the child that he or she is adopted, thereby obliterating the very existence of the birthparents. Worse, perhaps out of jealousy or anger, the adopting parents might tell the child that his or her biological parents were just like the terrible stereotypes of birthmothers, uncaring and irresponsible. Even the commitment to openness and possible later contact is risky for the birthparents. The agreement to maintain contact with each other is based solely on trust and is rarely legally enforceable. If they are cut off from the child by the adopting parents, the birthparents have no recourse. They will be left to spend the rest of their lives in the dark about their biological child, just what they risked so much to avoid.

Most adoptive parents are shocked that the birthparents have such fears. For their part, the birthparents are also surprised that the adopting couples worry that they will change their minds.

❖ I simply was not going to hurt Tim and Marina [the adopting parents] by changing my mind. I made that decision over a long period. I didn't just wake up one day and say, "Oh I think I will do this." I knew adoption was the best thing all along. Even though I can legally change my mind, that is not the issue. I just wouldn't do it. My baby has a good home. I mean that would be tearing her apart from her home and I wouldn't do that. I know that Tim and Marina are going to worry until everything is finally done. I only wish I could find some way to totally reassure them that they do not need to worry.

❖ When our birthmother, Molly, first came here to stay with us, the movie *Immediate Family* [about an open adoption of sorts] had just come out. I thought she and I should go see it together. All my friends said it would be a mistake to do that and thought I was crazy. We went and, of course, Molly and I both cried during the movie. But what really sticks out in my mind is how mad she was about the birthmother in the movie taking the baby back. Molly kept saying, "How could that girl do that? She said she was going to give the baby up, they had this agreement, she'd been living with them. And she had gone through so much to make that decision. I could never do that, never!"

What surprises and impresses most adoptive parents is that the birthparents' commitment to the adoption is as great as their own.

At the Birth

*T*he most trying part of the adoption process is probably the birth of the child. The birthparents are faced with making a final decision about their child. For the adopting parents, this is the moment of truth, as well: the time when they will find out if they are truly going to get the baby. This can be a time when feelings of jealousy are their most intense. For the birthparents, there is their envy of the fact that adopting parents, not they, are in a place to be able to raise their child. For the adopting parents, they see occurring right before their eyes the childbirth that they had hoped would be theirs.

In about 2 to 3 percent of the cases, the adoptive parents' worst nightmare comes true and the birthmother refuses to give them the baby. Most often, the birthmother has not changed her mind about the adoption but has been pressured to alter her decision by her family or the birthfather. Perhaps her parents suddenly offer her financial and emotional support or threaten serious reprisals. Maybe the birthfather now says he wants to be an active father and to get married. Occasionally the birthmother or birthfather simply cannot face the loss. In most cases, if a qualified open adoption counselor has been involved, the prospective adopting parents have been warned that this was likely to happen. But there are situations when the birthmother's decision comes as a surprise to everyone.

The wonder and power of open adoption is that such tragedies rarely happen. In fact, what most often averts this tragedy are the very bonds that have developed between adopting parents and birthparents.

❖ After our first bad experience, we decided that we weren't going to focus on the baby this time. We wanted to like the birthmom since the possibility existed for a relationship for thirty to fifty years. We thought it was important to like her for herself, not just the baby.

With Amber, we sensed a very important relationship building and it was like magic. It felt right and we wanted it. We didn't know that was going to happen until we started giving to the relationship. I am a firm believer that what goes in comes back. And this time everything worked and we have our wonderful daughter.

For the birthparents, the grief and pain of their decision is real but they can also see and feel the extraordinary joy they are bringing to the adopting parents, people about whom they have come to care so deeply.

❖ Whenever the pain really hit me, whenever the doubts hit me, I just kept thinking of Jim and Jessica and how much I loved them. I just know they will be wonderful parents because I know how they were with me. I am so glad I could bring that joy into their lives.

❖ I saw how much they wanted a baby and how much they could provide and that helped with my decision. I wouldn't change anything if I were to do it all over again, I mean get pregnant and everything. The whole thing has been such a positive experience for me that I would do it again. Well, maybe not.

Through the birth experience, the birthparents express most dramatically their certainty that the adopting parents, not themselves, are to be the baby's parents.

❖ Somehow, I still hung onto the myth that if Rhonda [our birthmother] saw the baby she would change her mind. He was such a cute baby. Rhonda looked lovingly down at the infant and then reached out to place him in *my* arms, saying "What do you think of *your* son?"

❖ As we stood there holding this incredible bundle of joy, we could hear Delores [the birthmother] calling for us to bring the baby in to see her in the room where they had taken her until the medication wore off. We knew better, but we still thought for a minute, "Oh no, maybe she changed her mind." When we got to her room, Delores took the baby in her arms and said, "I just wanted to be sure your daughter looked healthy." She said the "*your* daughter" part as if it was the most natural thing in the world to say.

❖ It felt so natural for me to be with our birthmother. We had spent a lot of time together. My husband had been working and I had already taken off work, so it was Kerry and I who formed the relationship. In fact, we were talking away when the baby popped out. She just said, "Well, Mom, you got your son." She started to cry and I started to cry, and we told each other all the things that we wanted for each other. Then she went off and had her tubal ligation. And I went off to check out my son. It was just wonderful.

❖ We went over to the house to pick up our adopted son. I remember everything on the drive over. It was one of those times you remember the rest of your life. There were lots of tears and hugging. It was really a very emotional moment for all of us when she handed over the baby to us and said, "Here is your son." And that is just the way she said it: "Here is your son."

❖ I was so tired after Kyle [my birthson] was born, I was just exhausted. Janet and Tim were there with me the whole time I was in the hospital, taking care of him, changing his diapers. From the very beginning, I wanted them to be mom and dad. I wasn't going to change any diapers or do any feedings, that was their job. I had just done my part and now it was their turn. They were so excited about it. They were just really cute. I was like "Bye, bye, go away, and let me sleep."

❖ Yes, I brought him [her birthson] into the world, but I know in my heart that parenting isn't just a physical thing, it is a relationship between people. I believed that the parents were out there somewhere, but that it wasn't me. I believe that I wasn't meant to raise this child. I was meant to give birth to him but someone else was meant to raise him.

❖ It was eight o'clock in the evening, the day after Sarah, our adopted daughter, was born. Visiting hours were over. There was a hospital guard who came to each room to make all the visitors leave. He came into the room and, of course, assumed that Jim was the father. But I appeared to be only a visitor so he asked me to leave. I asked why. He said that visiting hours were over. I said we had permission, and I tried to explain the whole adoption situation to him. He said we had to leave no matter what: visiting hours were over and only "real" parents could stay. Sandy, our birthmother, a strong-willed young woman, looked up at the guard from her bed, pointed to me, and said, quite forcefully, "She *is* the mother and he *is* the father and that is that!" The guard quickly left the room.

The Joy of an Adopted Child's Birth

A dopting parents deserve to have the same wonderful experience of birth as biological parents. The bonds that develop in most open adoptions make this possible. I have seen it over and over again. The room is filled with feelings of caring and love not only between parents and child but between adopting parents and birthparents as well.

❖ I came out of the delivery room and told Jim, my husband, that he had a son. I also told the birthgrandfather at the same time—and he hugged me. I'll never forget those moments.

❖ The hospital experience was probably the most beautiful thing that I have ever had happen to me in my life. Right up until the moment on the day of birth Marty had told us that she wanted us there but she wasn't really sure that she wanted us in the labor room with her. We got a call one night about eleven o'clock from Marty's mother, who said they were at the hospital and we'd better get up there because she was going to have it fast. She didn't say anything about whether she was going to have us in the delivery room or not, but when we got there that was the end of it. We went into the delivery room—it was more like a bedroom with a lot of space—a little after midnight. She gave birth about nine in the morning after a pretty tough labor. Up until the very end, Marty was laughing and joking and it was extraordinary.

This sharing of the profound experience of birth also lays the groundwork for a lifetime of connection.

❖ Mary Beth, the birthmother of our adopted child, is one unique woman. Because of her and our good match, Gary and I have had one of the most remarkable experiences of our lives! While the five weeks Mary Beth was here were a bit long for all of us (at times), we had a chance to really get to know her, and for that we are especially grateful. It's so nice to know that when Robbie asks about his mom, we can tell him all about her and how wonderful she is. The last two days Mary Beth was here were especially heartwarming as the three of us shared laughs over good times and tears over Mary Beth's departure.

❖ The birth is such a mixture of feelings. You are elated because you are receiving an incredible gift of life but, on the other hand, you know the birthparents are going through such loss. There is a powerful bonding that comes from sharing that experience.

❖ We were at the birth but our birthmother wanted to wait a few days and then meet us in the park to give us our new baby. We met at this wonderful park where my grandfather used to feed the birds. We talked for about an hour and then our birthmother, Priscilla, looked at her watch and said, "Well, it's time to go." Dave and I just thought, "Oh, God, how is this going to work?" But she just got up and wrapped the baby, and then we all walked to the car. She bent over the baby and put him into our car seat. We gave her a hug and she said, "Call me when you get home." Then she walked away. It was clear that this was hard for her to do that but she had made up her mind. She is so mature. When I talk to her now it's like talking to a peer of mine even though she is only twenty years old.

Until the Adoption Is Finalized

What about the weeks and sometimes months that have to pass before an adoption is final under the law? Adoption laws vary state by state, but the paperwork is rarely completed in less than six months; eight to nine months is more common. People wonder if they will be able to fully enjoy being new parents when the possibility of the birthparents taking the child back seems to hang like a sword over their heads.

Of course, most adopting parents are relieved when the court completes the final papers. Needless to say, this is especially the case when the adoption is a risky one. What helps, though, is the openness of the process. In contrast to various forms of closed adoptions, there is no mystery about the identity and character of the birthparents or why they are having their child adopted. Because the adopting parents know so much about the lives and concerns of the birthparents, they also know the terrible impact taking the baby back would have on the birthparents'—especially the birthmother's—plans and hopes for their lives.

There are also more mundane forces at work in these early months. There is so much to be concerned about in taking care of a newborn—adjusting work and sleep schedules, worrying about the baby's health, dealing with diaper rash, or wondering whether the child is eating or sleeping enough. There is little time for worry about the birthparents changing their minds.

> ❖ I had this fantasy that when I took the baby home, I would put bars on the door, turn off all the lights after 6:00, and refuse to answer my phone. All out of fear of the birthmother, of course. The reality was so different. Who had time for these things? I was too busy with bottles, diapers, calls to the doctor, and trying to get some sleep. And when I was not busy like that, I was busy being thrilled with watching every little thing my baby was doing. It is not that I never thought about her taking the baby back. I did sometimes and when I did I was scared. I called our counselor or even the birthmother and soon got back on track. But mostly, I was too busy being a mother to be concerned.

Sometimes, though, the bond between adopting parents and birthparents is so powerful that the inconceivable happens—the couple is almost reluctant to take the child. They feel so close to her that they share in her sense of loss.

❖ Theresa [the birthmother] is not a crier. I mean she went through over twenty-one hours of labor without a whimper. So when she came over to visit the baby a few days after the birth and burst into tears, it tore us apart. I felt like I was a schizophrenic or something. I wanted the baby but I was feeling so much grief for Theresa. I mean your friend is going through an awful time but you're the one who is going to get this baby. When she left, she was crying and we were devastated. We were both sobbing. I wanted a baby but I never wanted it at anybody's expense and I felt like she was really suffering.

Thank God, Theresa called us a little while later. She called and said, "This is not a long call. I am just calling to tell you that I am okay and that I am worried about *you.* I am worried that you guys are going to be so concerned about me, it's going to overshadow your joy of being new parents and you're not going to really get in there. I just want you to know that everything is okay. I'm very emotional, my hormones have kicked in but I am okay and I want you to be really happy and excited."

It is strange to say, but we were more concerned about our birthmother than about the baby.

What seems to work best in these early months is maintaining the same level of caring and trust that has been carefully built before the birth.

❖ We found out months later that one of the most important experiences for Marti [the birthmother] was when we brought the baby up to see her when he was just nine days old. Our willingness to visit then showed her that we had built a relationship on trust, not fear. We had started with a very honest relationship and though we were scared sometimes, we followed through.

And she did as well. At the end of the visit, when she helped load him back into the car again, it was like, "Well, I'll see you later" and off we went. Only nine days after our son was born and here we were having another beautiful experience with his birthmother. It just cemented further for us that the right things were happening and that these are the right things to be doing.

6

The Ongoing Relationships Between Adopting Parents and Birthparents

Once the adoption is completed, what happens to the relationship between adopting parents and birthparents? It is one thing to relate to a birthmother (and birthfather) for the three to six months before the birth and a few months until the adoption is finalized. But an ongoing, perhaps lifetime, relationship is something else again. Adopting couples are concerned that the birthparents may be troublesome and full of lifelong problems they must help solve. What if the birthparents are intrusive, critical of how the adopting parents are raising the child, and constantly reminding them—intentionally or not—that the birthparents are the "true" parents?

These fears are both understandable and reasonable. After all, the idea of a connection between birthparents and adopting parents that might last a lifetime is new to most people.

And there are some situations in which these relationships can become a burden for the adoptive family. Fortunately, most open adoption programs report that clients find these postbirth relationships not only surprisingly easy but enjoyable and valuable.

The Postbirth Relationship

*T*o begin with, adding a new relative to the family is not a process unique to adoption. Marriage, after all, adds not only a spouse to the family but a whole new set of relatives as well. After the wedding, there are all these additional aunts, uncles, brothers-in-law, cousins, nephews, and nieces. Typically, some of these new relatives are likable, and others are troublesome. Sometimes, people have a favorite aunt or uncle with whom they have so much in common that they become close friends. Other relatives remain just relatives. Some families are unusually tight-knit and have a strong sense of a family. Others may be separated by physical distance, by differences in life-style, or just by a sense of being more private about their lives. Nevertheless, even distant relatives get greeting cards on holidays and pictures of the children. The expansion of family obligations through marriage is expected, normal, and routine.

Most adoptive parents report that adding birthparents to their family is like expanding their family through marriage. Some find it easier to relate to a birthparent than some of their own relations or in-laws. In an open adoption, the adopting parents actively *choose* the birthparents themselves, while most other relatives come by birth or marriage, not by choice. In some cases, adopting parents find that they have more in common with the birthparents than with some of their own relatives. After all, the adopting parents and birthparents have selected each other because of their similarities in values and outlook. They also share something of enormous consequence in common: the adopted child.

As with regular families, there is considerable diversity in the relationships between adopting parent and birthparents. Some adopting parents are in regular contact with their birthparents. Others see the birthparents only on rare occasions. The frequency of contact depends partly on logistics—such as distance apart or busy life-styles—and partly on how much the adopting parents and birthparents like each other. Some birthparents visit infrequently, while others visit often. We even had one birthmother who baby-sat for the adopting couple. But that intimate a relationship was by the adopting parents' *own choice.* A more typical scenario is that the birthparents visit or, more often, call once or twice a month during the first few months after the birth. Later, this contact drops to once a month, then later to every few months, and finally to once a year or less. Again, the analogy with relatives is apt. When there is a new baby in the family, most close relatives will initially visit often to see the cute new addition. There is something irresistible about an infant. But gradually, the visits become less frequent.

In some open adoptions, just as in some families, these relationships do not go smoothly. The birthparents may use poor judgment, perhaps calling too often, being habitually late for visits, making inappropriate comments to the adopting parents of the child, or missing important counseling appointments. What happens in these cases is the same thing that happens when any relative treats another family member rudely. Everyone tries hard to work out the problem and to remember that they are all still "family." Counseling can help smooth over the rough spots. But if the problems cannot be solved, the adopting parents and birthparents end up breaking contact with each other altogether.

❖ We wanted to have an open, ongoing relationship with our child's birthfather because we liked him and knew how important that would be for Dan, our son. But the same thing kept happening time after time. Jack [the birthfather] would call and tell us how much he wanted to see Dan. We would invite him over and then he would not show up at the time we agreed on. Often, we had to make special arrangements to see him, and when he was a no-show, it was a big deal. And he never once called us to tell us he was not coming or to say he was sorry.

Finally, we just had to tell him that we could not put up with that anymore. Youth or no youth, there was no excuse for this. We told him that the next time he was a no-show, he shouldn't bother calling us for six months.

There can be problems from the other direction as well. Sometimes adopting parents treat the birthparents inconsiderately. They may keep forgetting to send cards or photos they agreed to send. They may fail to honor their agreement to a certain number of visits per year.

❖ I do not agree about your decision to stop having Marjorie and me [the birthparents] visit Matthew until he specifically tells you he wants us to visit. I thought we were all pretty clear about what we agreed on. I am clear that you are Matt's parents and he is solely your responsibility, but I still feel bad that you are changing the agreement at this late date. I am worried that this will make us the "mystery people." The whole idea of open adoption is that the more Matthew knows us— including seeing us in person—the less of a possible threat we will be to him or to you.

These misunderstandings can be a source of terrible pain

and anguish to all of those involved, especially the child. Fortunately, there is often counseling and mediation help available through the counselors that facilitated the adoption in the first place.

In actuality, as with so many of the areas of potential conflict in open adoption, almost everyone involved in this process finds that such postadoption problems are not only unusual, but rare. Before the birth, most adopting parents and birthparents have developed an extraordinarily strong bond, a sense of mutual respect and caring, that continues after the birth. From the point of view of the adoptive parents, whatever fears and hesitancies are left typically melt away as the adoptive parents experience the intensity of being new mothers and fathers.

❖ All our fears—and we had a lot—were really coming out of the fact that we did not have the baby we wanted so badly. That's what made us so nervous, so one down, so scared, so distrustful and distant sometimes from the birthmother. Once we had our baby—and she was our baby the moment we looked at her—we relaxed, we were satisfied, the world no longer looked scary. And neither did Terri, our birthmother.

❖ If I do my job as the father, why should I be afraid of my child loving somebody more than me? I just do my job and have my own relationship with the child. As time goes on, whatever the future has for Jolene [the birthmother] and Amelia [the adopted daughter], you know they will come to their own level on their own terms later. And that doesn't jeopardize or threaten the security of my family.

From the birthparents' point of view, they have made their peace with the fact that their child is being raised by somebody else. They see for themselves that their child is an integral part of a loving, caring, stable family. To disrupt that family would mean, as one birthmother explained, "disrupting my dream of a happy home for my child." Besides, if the birthparents' connection with the adoptive family is severed, that means never knowing what happens to their child.

For both the adoptive parents and birthparents, a positive relationship is important for the child's sake above all. It is an affirmation that the child's adoption was caring, loving, and normal.

What Are These Relationships Like?

*T*here are many variations and dimensions to the relationships between adoptive parents and birthparents. Sometimes the usual roles are even reversed: the birthparents become the ones who provide badly needed support to the adopting parents.

❖ Gina [the birthmother] asked me [the adopting mom] if I would bring her birthson—age two months—for a visit. I said yes, but as the day approached, I started to panic. I called Eileen, my adoption counselor. She reassured me that Gina was deeply committed to the adoption but also suggested that I openly share my fears with the birthmother. The morning for the visit arrived and I felt like I just could not go through with it. I called Gina and told her what was going on, just as Eileen had suggested. She said, "Get real, Maria, I'm not taking Jeff back and you know it, damn it! Just get down here so I can see YOU play with him and hug him and kiss him and know how happy he is. Okay??" For months, I—her senior by twenty years—had been the one to help Gina. She was the one who needed emotional support. Sud-

denly we had switched roles. It was Gina who took control of the situation in that wonderful way that only
young people can.

❖ I felt fine about Lorena's adoption, but my mother was
in a state of panic worrying that Lisa, the birthmother,
would take her granddaughter away. Nothing I said
seemed to reassure her. I mentioned this one day to Lisa,
not meaning that this was in any way her responsibility.
It wasn't her problem, really. Lisa did not say anything
at the time, but a few days later, I found out she called
my mother herself. After a little chitchat, she had told
my mother, "Mrs. Bergson, I just want you to know that
what I want more than almost anything in the world is
for *you* to be Lorena's grandmother. Okay?" That was
just what my mother needed to hear.

What is striking to many open adoption counselors is that
the connection that develops over the years between the
adopting parents and birthparents is not just centered on the
child. The relationship is between them as people.

❖ When you become parents of a newborn, you disappear
in everybody's eyes. When people come for a visit, they
don't really want to see you, they want to see the baby.
People will walk over to you in a room and look right
past you and start talking or looking at the baby. Babies
have that power. It's okay, but you do feel a little funny
about it sometimes. That is what made it so special when
Wendy, our birthmother, told us that it was harder for
her to leave us than it was to leave the baby. I still call
her every Saturday. Usually when she calls she asks
about what I'm doing and what Dennis is doing, rather
than about the baby. Oh, she does ask about the baby,
but she's more concerned about us.

❖ Three months after Lilly was born, we went to visit
her birthmother. We were scared about going down

there. When we got there, she said to us right away, "You know, I'd like to see the baby. But, if you don't mind too much, most of all I want to see you guys." Wow, that was nice.

❖ When I go to see them [the adopting parents], it is not just to see my daughter, but also a lot to see Barbara and Don. Even if Michele hadn't been the reason we came together, I know we would have hit it off and we would have had a relationship anyway. They are really special people.

It is important to me to think about them and their feelings. For instance, the day of the final adoption I knew they were going to be terrified to call me. Everyone thinks the birthmother is going to be crushed. Well I was waiting around all day for them to call me and nothing happened. So I called them and I said, congratulations, tell me everything. I wanted to hear it all because they were my friends and I wanted to hear how their day went. That is what it is all about, sharing our joy about Michele.

Sometimes the connection is primarily between the adoptive mother and the birthmother. The adoptive mother frequently feels motherly toward the birthmother and seeks out or welcomes this closeness. From the birthmother's point of view, the adopting mother is an older adult who knows all about her, someone to whom she can talk about intimate problems but who is not her own overprotective or critical mother. Many people have these types of nonparent adult friends or relatives when they are young, and they often play an important role in their lives. When this kind of intimate relationship develops in open adoption, we find, the adopting mother and birthmother may talk every week, but the topics for discussion rarely concern the adopted child. More often than not, they talk about the usual challenges and problems of a young woman in our society. This means a great deal to the birthmother and the adoptive mother as well.

> ❖ I often talk two and three times a week to Paula [our birthmother]. But, you know, though we are so connected through the adoption of our son, Paul, we almost never talk about him. What we chat about are social things. Like lately, we keep talking about this guy she's madly in love with. He's a premed student and she doesn't know what to do since she's just a freshman in college. After all, getting serious about a medical student seems a pretty heavy decision with all those years of school ahead of him. She knows that I put my husband, Dave, through medical school and she wants some advice from me. She wants a lot of advice, actually. We talk for hours about this stuff, and, to tell the truth, I love it. Partially, it's reliving my life, partially it's like being an older sister. Besides, I really love Paula.

Does this mean that open adoption requires taking care of someone in her (or his) teen or postteen years? It's not unheard of for adoptive parents to feel as if they have taken on the burden of raising a problem teenager. And since young people can be very needy—probably a standard part of adolescence—this can be quite a chore. But such situations are unusual. First, most birthparents are in their early twenties and are not teenagers. Second, when the adopting parents assume some burden of emotional support for a young birthparent, they do so by choice, not obligation. If they are unsympathetic or simply have no time to help, the birthmother typically gets the message and stops asking for help when it becomes clear she is not going to get any.

Some adoptive parents are apprehensive that the birthparents will become a nuisance over the years. Will they be critical of everything from the adoptive parents' decision about whether to use cloth diapers or disposable diapers to the choice of public school for their child? Initially, I shared those same concerns and expected that a considerable amount of counseling time might have to be spent on resolving these issues. But that has not been the case. To the surprise of both adoptive parents and adoption professionals, few such problems arise. But that should not be surprising. If the birthparents wanted any kind of ongoing involvement with the child, they could have taken the easier path and kept the child. Instead, they searched hard for people they could feel confident would be the best possible parents for their baby so that they could leave all those problems to the child's new parents.

> ❖ Sandy visited a lot right at first but it was comfortable. We had only met her a month ahead of time but we love her, she has given us the greatest gift she ever could. She was clear how she felt about the adoption. She was adopted so she had that perspective. Her visits gradually got less and less. At first, when she came over, she would offer to feed him or change him. But soon, when he needed feeding and another diaper, she would say "you do it."

As I mentioned earlier, there can be postadoption problems, even serious ones, between adoptive parents and birthparents. Yet the overwhelming number of postadoption counseling issues that do arise are not about the birthparents wanting *too much* contact but wanting *too little*. Sometimes the pain and grief of having had their child adopted will make birthparents stay away or cut themselves off for months or even years. Sometimes, one or both birthparents disappear simply because young people are so mobile these days. When suddenly cut off in this way, adoptive parents often feel hurt for themselves and for their child.

> ❖ No, we don't feel threatened by the birthparents. Actually, to tell you the truth, we used to see our birthmother every four to six weeks. Now she is off doing something else so we have not seen her for over a

year. We feel pretty bad that she has not called in so long.

❖ What really hurt was when Jackie [the birthmother] started cutting herself off from us. Before we began this process, we used to worry that she would be around too much. How different it is now. Now we worry that she might drop right out of our lives altogether. She is such an extraordinary young woman and we have shared so much with her. How will we explain to Timmy that the woman who loved him so much that she chose adoption, rather than abortion or single parenting has now disappeared? And we miss her!

❖ Interestingly enough—and I think this is what most adoptive parents will find—our birthmother is the one who started pulling back and not us. She is the one who started saying, "Gee, I am starting to get on with my life so please stay in touch with my family but I am not sure I want to get calls all the time." We have respected that and I am still in touch with her mom on a real regular basis. But I feel bad about it.

This issue arose recently when we requested feedback from our adopting parents at the center about possible changes in one of the special forms we use called the Open Adoption Agreement. The handout helps adopting parents and birthparents to discuss and agree on certain specifics such as the role the adoptive parents will play at the time of the labor and delivery or who will call whom first, after the baby goes home from the hospital. More general issues, too, are addressed such as what type of contact will be maintained over the years. When we asked adopting parents whether they wanted to add any provisions to keep the birthparents at a greater distance, the answer was a resounding "No!" On the contrary, most parents wanted the agreement to specify that birthparents stay in touch with the adopting parents on a regular basis. At the very least, they wanted the birthparents to notify the adopting parents—or at least the counselors—once a year about how they could be reached.

Normal and Special at the Same Time

*A*s time goes by, these close relationships between the adoptive parents and birthparents become almost casual or routine, just as they would be in a biological family. The sense of normalcy is striking. In the initial stages of any important social change, the new social relationships that emerge still seem exotic and unusual. Once those changes have taken root in the society, the roles that once appeared unnatural now seem natural and hardly worthy of notice anymore. This is exactly what happens in most open adoption families. Sometimes, one of our adopting couples will tell me matter-of-factly, "Oh yes, we had our birthmother over for Christmas dinner," or "Just the other day, our birthmother and her new boyfriend came over and we got a baby-sitter and all went out to a movie," or "The birthgrandfather was in town the other day on business and he came by to see Jackie, our daughter. It was nice." What always impresses me is the couple's genuine fondness as they talk about their birthparents. The tone is the same one people use when they speak of a favorite cousin or nephew or the son of one of their old college friends. Both the content and style of these stories always make me smile. The adopting parents are talking about what might seem revolutionary occurrences by closed adoption standards. For most open adoption families, though, these are just a normal and routine part of their everyday lives.

❖ We had been through seven years of every imaginable infertility treatment to no avail, but now, through adoption, we have our beautiful little girl, Samantha. Since we felt close to Samantha's birthparents, we asked them both if they wanted to come to the annual picnic for adoptive families. Jamie, the birthmother, needed some distance and so declined the offer, but Bill, the birthfather, accepted.

We met Bill at the picnic and had a good time. As the picnic came to a close, we started to pack up to leave but realized that we had more stuff to take back to the car than we could possibly carry. As any parent knows, it takes a lot of hardware and assorted goodies to go to a picnic with a baby: stroller, car seat, diapers, bottles, baby food, toys, bibs, and more. So we decided we would carry all the stuff and have Bill carry Samantha.

To outsiders, the scene of all of us all walking together to the car might have seemed shocking. After all, here was the birthfather, not the adopting parents, carrying the baby. But that's not how this felt to us. To us, it was just the most efficient way to get to our car.

Yet the casualness of these relationships should not obscure the depth of the connections. Almost everyone approaches open adoption with apprehensions about their relationship with birthmothers and birthfathers. They often begin the process without having resolved those doubts. But, in the end, most adopting parents find their relationship with their child's birthparents to be one of their greatest treasures.

❖ When we first learned about open adoption, I think we had the same fears everybody else has. An open adoption is something you don't feel really comfortable with at first. You worry that somebody else is going to tell you how to bring up your kid, and that she is going to be visiting all the time since she knows exactly where you live. I think my original thoughts were more of a child as a possession than they are now. Having known the birthmother for ten months, I just can't go back and logically think why I ever had those fears. She is not interested in telling me how to raise the child. Even if she were, she wouldn't get anywhere with me anyway and she knows that. And we enjoy having her around. I think as you learn to trust the birthmother, your fears quickly disappear.

❖ I was the one most scared of open adoption. I went through the phone book and called every agency, and by the end I was sure open adoption was not for me. And now, we are convinced that it is best for everyone. It makes it much easier on our daughter. She will know where she comes from and why. We have all her medical records and we can get more information, anytime, if anything ever comes up. It has been just wonderful. We have a real great relationship with her birthmother. Like having more family.

As the months have gone by, the visits have become less frequent because our birthmother is involved in her own life. She is engaged to be married and has a five-year-old son whom she had when she was seventeen. We saw her a couple of days ago—we went with her and some other adopting couples to the local zoo, along with her fiancé and her son.

❖ I wanted to ask the counselors if feeling so strongly about our birthmother is normal, even so many months after the birth. I still find myself bragging about her to all my friends. I hope this is not too unusual.

❖ When we first found out that our birthmother, Miranda, lived in Atlanta, almost three thousand miles away, we were pleased. We liked the idea that she was so far away. Now it's two years later and I can tell you the distance makes us very sad. My company sent me to a conference in Atlanta a few months ago. I put in the minimum time I needed at the conference and then spent every possible hour at Miranda's house for visits and talks. What a delightful time we had together.

❖ This is really embarrassing. When I was at an open adoption orientation eighteen months ago, the counselor talked about how close we would probably get to our birthmother. He said we probably would not believe him at that time, but someday we would. I looked over at my husband and we exchanged a look that said, "He's got that right: we don't believe him."

And here I am, two years later, feeling so close to our birthmother and having to admit that he was right—and worse, that the guy can even say "told you so."

❖ Our initial vision was that we would know the birthmom a little and maybe we would see her once or twice a year. Hopefully less. Now we enjoy Marta's company so much and we are so fond of her. She is part of our lives and part of our son's life. We are closer to her than we are with some of the other members of our family.

❖ Tammy, our daughter Stephanie's birthmother, came to visit us for four days in May, over Mother's Day weekend. My mom was here on a visit at the same time, which was really nice since they had never met each other before. Tammy arrived on a Saturday, and it felt just like a cousin or dear friend we hadn't seen in a long time was here to visit. We hadn't seen her in almost three years, since our daughter was about thirteen months old.

We had a nice Mother's Day and Tammy's parents even called and wished us all well. Stephanie has nursery school Tuesday and Thursday and the moms take turns volunteering to help the teachers. The Tuesday that Tammy was here, she went to help out at the school in my place. And I think she really enjoyed it. We are really glad that she resumed contact with us again.

❖ We have some friends who are going through an adoption now. When they found out about our situation, they said, "I don't think this is for us." Once they met their birthmother, everything changed. They couldn't wait for her to come and stay with them for a while.

For many adopting couples, the open adoption process is so compelling that they refuse to accept anything less in subsequent adoptions.

❖ When we got a call from a birthmother for our second adoption, we had to turn her down. She sounded like a lovely young woman but she lived in a small town in the South. We knew that once we adopted her child, we probably would never see her [the birthmother] again. We feel so close to our first birthmother—who lives only a few towns over—that we just could not imagine having a birthmother with whom we had so little contact. Now understand, we are just regular folks, not your California "touchie-feelies" or anything like that. We just knew that we wanted a birthmother who lived closer.

❖ A birthmother called us after talking to a counselor. She seemed terrific but she was not willing to meet us in person. It was one of the hardest things I ever did, but I had to tell her that if we couldn't meet her in person, we just could not do it. We'd been waiting over a year for our second adoption and we knew we might lose her. But we just had to take the chance. We were that convinced in our hearts about open adoption.

If many adopting parents are surprised by the depth of these relationships, so are many of the birthparents. The potential barriers between adopting parents and birthparents go both ways. Birthparents can feel considerable distance, antipathy, and jealousy toward the adopting parents. In a sense, the adopting parents have everything the birthparents want: financial stability, a successful marriage, and *even* their baby. And many birthparents do feel these emotions. When they cannot get beyond them, the relationship with the adoptive parents becomes hostile, cold, or constrained. But just as the initial fears and jealousies of many adoptive parents give way, so do those of most birthparents.

TO REBECCA, MY BIRTHDAUGHTER

They came into our lives so full of love,
They must have been sent from God above.

They are the best friends that I've ever had
These people you know as Mom and Dad.

I knew from the start, that come what may,
I could trust these people not to take you away.

For all that has happened, they always knew
How much love I would always have for you.

I knew they were our miracle—And we were theirs too,
Inspired by the love we all had for you.

❖ Hi. I'm just sitting here thinking about Ken and Patty and how lucky I am. I am graduating on June eighth with my class and all of my friends—something I know I could not have done had I kept Sean. Both Sean and I have chances for incredible futures due largely to all of your caring. I will never be able to thank you enough.

The three of them (Ken, Patti, and Sean) are coming up here next week for my graduation. He is the sweetest baby and when I see them together as a family, I can't help but smile and be happy for them. I know that one day, when I'm grown up, I'll have my turn. Right now, though, I'm just glad that we've all got a chance: Ken and Patti to have a family, Sean to be loved and cherished by two parents who were ready for the responsibility, and me, lucky enough still to be a part of his life and yet also be young for a while longer.

7

The Lives of an Adopted Child and Adoptive Parents in an Open Adoption

*I*f open adoption is primarily about relationships, what about the most important relationship of all: the bonds between the adopting parents and their adopted child? People want to know about the impact of openness on the health and stability of the adopted family.

Many of the concerns of adoptive parents are not unique to adoption. Starting and maintaining a family can be intimidating to almost anybody, not just adopting parents. If they are young, many new parents worry that they are too inexperienced. Men and women who become parents at any age older than customary may wonder if they will have enough energy to be active mothers and fathers. Perhaps they are too set in their ways to make the adjustments necessary to become good parents. Parenthood is, after all, a leap into the unknown. Few people receive any training or preparation for becoming a mother or father, yet parenthood is a complicated, ever-changing, and lifetime undertaking. The only model available to most couples is their own parents, and often people are hesitant about following that example too closely. Even if the new mother and father plan to build on the model of their parents, the task is not easy. Most people don't know, for example, how their parents felt as parents, or what was behind their actions or decisions. How did their parents decide how to discipline their children, when to toilet train, or what the role of religion in the family should be?

Becoming a parent through open adoption raises additional concerns. After years of unsuccessful attempts to have a child, many men and women worry that they will have a hard time being adequate parents even under the best of conditions. Will their children be painfully confused by seeming to have two sets of parents? Will they themselves ever feel like true parents if the birthparents are always in the picture?

❖ I wanted a baby so much and open adoption seemed right. But could I ever feel like the true mother if there was someone out there with a claim to motherhood based on biology? And wouldn't it make it even harder if I kept acknowledging that claim through letters or even contacts between us and the birthparents, or even worse, the birthparents and our child?

In some ways the research on adopted children is not very encouraging. Studies of closed adoption point out the all-too-frequent problems that procedure can create (see chapter 2). Long-term studies of impact of open adoption are not yet available since this procedure is relatively new. It may be another twenty years before researchers can finally and absolutely certify that open adoption works.

How, then, can prospective adopting parents decide the best way to create their families? Obviously they cannot wait for another twenty years until the final research is in. In the end, all they can do is look at current information about the positive impact of open adoption on children and parents and make their decisions on that basis.

Fortunately, there is a great deal of evidence that open adoption not only works but brings stability and joy to all of those involved in the process. Throughout this book, I have tried to show that the fears about open adoption simply do not come to pass for most people. Nowhere is this more true than with the impact of open adoption on the normal lives of adoptive parents and their children.

The Adopted Child's Heritage

As it should be, the greatest benefactor in an open adoption is the child. In the past, a child's adoption was, at best, a source of confusion and doubt. At worst, it was a source of shame. What a contrast with open adoption. The child knows all the details of his or her biological origins. Most important, the child knows that the adoption was a healthy, caring, and loving process. The fact of their adoption is not kept secret; instead their adoption is openly discussed with pride and joy.

Through open adoption, children have access to the same information about their origins that nonadopted children take for granted. They know the names of their biological parents, their nationality, their health history, and their hometowns. But they have more than just the cold facts. Children often respond better to stories and pictures than a straightforward presentation of information. With open adoption, the adoptive parents can tell their child about his or her adoption as a special family story. They can talk about why and how they decided to become adopting parents, how they met their daughter's or son's birthparents, what happened in the months before the birth, and how all of them shared in the child's birth. Young children love to hear the same story repeated often, especially if they are included in the tale. In open adoption, just as in biological birth, the story of the child's arrival into the family becomes a part of the family folklore.

As part of this heritage, most adopting parents create an album of photographs and mementos of the adoption. They show this often to their child and to friends and relatives as well. There are usually numerous photos of the birthparents and of the first meetings and get-togethers of the adopting parents and birthparents. There are pictures of the birthmother during her pregnancy and of all of them at the hospital for the child's birth. Often these albums include the open adoption version of their child's birth announcement, which instead of mentioning only the adoptive parents, tells the whole story.

The proud and frequent display of this album is an important assurance to a child of the positive nature of the adoption. Even before they are old enough to understand what adoption means technically, the children of open adoption associate adoption-related words and phrases with excitement and joy.

❖ One evening at dinner, we asked our son, Jacob, whether he was adopted. Jacob is two years old. He responded with an enormous smile and a look of pride and a "Yes, I am adopted." Then one of our dinner guests asked him if he knew what that meant. He said "No," matter-of-factly and calmly turned back to the toy he had been playing with. But his smile gave away that what he did know about his adoption was the important part—that it was something of joy.

❖ I sing my adopted daughter a song every night with her birthmother's name in it. She already uses the word *adopted* because we are going to try to adopt another baby. She will say, "Oh, Mom, are we going to adopt

♥

To Announce the Birth

May 10, 1991

of

Gabriella Martinez

8 lbs, 9 oz

In Seattle, Washington

♥

Born in Love

To Her Birthparents

Brian Nathanson

Gerri Bowdon

♥

Given in Love

To Her Adoptive Parents

Joe and Carol Martinez

another baby soon?" and I say, "Yes, that's right." It all seems normal for her.

❖ You would have to have been there to appreciate it fully. There was our five-year-old adopted daughter, Rebecca, with this big look of surprise on her face. She had just found out that her new friend, Jackie, did not have a birthmother (she was not adopted). What a turnaround from the old days. Instead of feeling bad that she was adopted and Jackie was not, Rebecca felt sorry for Jackie because she was *not* adopted and so did not have any birthmother.

An essential part of the adoption story is that the child's birthparents chose who would be his or her parents. If this choice had been made by a social worker, a lawyer, a counselor, or a doctor, it would carry little weight with most children. The status of these professionals is of little importance to young people. What matters to them is that this momentous decision was made by the same people who brought them into the world.

The adopted parents' own positive feelings about their children's birthparents play an important role here. All adopting parents—whether the adoption was open or closed—are going to have the good sense to talk in approving terms about their child's birthparents. But talking favorably is not a matter simply of using the right words and phrases. Most children are sensitive, not just to the specific content of what their parents say to them, but to the nuances and tone behind the words. What is reassuring to an adopted child is sensing the genuine caring the parents have for their birthparents, not just spoken approval. In a closed adoption, this can be difficult. The adopting parents know so little about the birthparents. Even in some open adoptions this can be a problem, especially if adequate counseling and support have not been available. If the adoption process was filled with distrust, anger, and misunderstanding, how effectively can the adopting parents convey a good feeling about the adoption to their child? An open adoption accompanied by good counseling paints a different picture. Because they have had such a thoughtful, close relationship with the birthparents, the adoptive mother and father have an easy time talking about them with familiarity, fondness, and respect.

Knowing Why Their Birthparents Chose to Have Them Adopted

Often the deepest concern of adopted children is *why* their birthparents chose to have them adopted. Was it a whimsical, casual decision—or worse, was it because of something bad about them, the adopted children? Or was their adoption based on love and genuine concern? An adopted child's sense of self-worth is deeply affected by the answer to these questions. Fortunately, with open adoption, there are powerful ways to reassure children that their birthparents made their decision from a sense of love, not rejection.

Many open adoption counselors, though not all, ask the birthparents to write a letter to their child explaining their decision. Some of these letters are a few pages in length, others are longer, and some are more like poems. The birthparents write about their concerns about becoming parents. They explain the reasons why they thought the best life for their child would come through adoption. They talk about why they were so sure that they had found the right new parents for their child. Instead of being hidden in some government or agency archives, the letters remain in the adoptive parents' personal possession to be shown to the child whenever they feel it is appropriate. When adoptive parents have these letters, they typically make them a part of the special adoption album that they regularly show to their child. Other parents choose to leave this letter out of the album and save it for when the child is older. Regardless of the timing, the letter can be an important affirmation to the child of the love of the biological parents. This is one example:

Dear Eric (my birthson):

I couldn't face the thought of bringing a baby into this world without a dad, without financial security, and without emotional stability. I was so scared for you, so confused. I decided that the best thing to do for you, Eric, was to give you life. Whatever happened, you were inside me and deserved the right to live. I started looking into the world of adoption. I hated it. It was too much like a business. If I were going to have someone else raise you, I wanted to meet them, get to know them. I wanted to love them before I let them love you. I was stumped until I was seven months along. That was when I met your parents, Mark and Melinda. I found a number in the paper for a place that helps girls who choose open adoption. It said all the choices were mine. I checked it out, and it was what I wanted for you.

My biggest fear, Eric, is that because of my decision to give a family to you, you may be bitter and angry. I never want you to feel I don't love you. I love you so very much—so very, very much.

When you were inside me I would cry and tell you how sorry I was for doing this to you. But as I look down at your perfect little face, I'm not sorry, Eric. How could I be sorry to give life to such a miracle?

Importance of Ongoing Contact

When it is possible, the actual presence of the birthparents in their lives can be the most profound form of reassurance to adopted children about the normalcy of their adoption. In fully open adoptions, the children have not only information about their birthparents but the opportunity to see and talk to them in person as well. Such contact can be quite important. Children—and perhaps adults as well—respond better to concrete, tangible information than to abstract words or concepts like *birthmother* or *extended family* or *open adoption*. And what could be more concrete for children than seeing their birthparents in person? What could be more powerful for adopted children than sitting on their birthmother's lap and feeling firsthand her love and caring? What could be more convincing that all is well than experiencing directly the caring between their adopting parents and their birthparents? The comfortable and almost casual involvement of the birthparents in the child's family—even if infrequent—can be a powerful affirmation of the positive and normal nature of the child's adoption.

The importance of this personal connection becomes apparent in cases where previously closed adoptions have been opened up. Typically, the family's first child was adopted through some type of closed and secretive process but the adoption of their second child was an open procedure. Having seen the advantages of openness, the adoptive parents want the same for their first child. Sometimes, this is just not possible: the records are completely inaccessible or the birthparent refuses to visit. More often, the birthparents are found, contact is made, and the results are uniformly positive.

❖ Jeff was a good kid but still he had some behavioral problems that were upsetting to us. And they were just starting to be a problem for his day-care teachers as well. Jeff's adoption had been a closed adoption through a traditional agency in the Midwest. Our second child, Jamie, was adopted through an open adoption, so we decided to open Jeff's closed adoption. After months and months of negotiation—to use a polite word—with the agency that had arranged Jeff's adoption, we finally got permission for Jeff to meet his birthmother. The agency insisted that the meeting happen in the agency's office and under its supervision. We agreed, since this was a step in the right direction at least. When Jeff met his birthmother, he was shy at first. Soon, though, he was talking to her a mile a minute about his toys, games, school, and his life. We just sat back and watched. It was wonderful. At the end, we promised to stay in touch and we have.

After that meeting, and others that followed, the change in Jeff was remarkable. He seemed more relaxed, self-confident. The sudden change in his behavior baffled his day-care teachers. Jeff was never a bad kid but suddenly he seemed like one of the mellowest boys.

❖ When she was seventeen years old, Margie chose us to be the parents of her child though the IAC. We were overjoyed and soon had our new baby, Jessica, in our home. We felt close to both Margie and her parents and, especially since they lived close, worked hard to keep our connection with them.

Four or five years ago, Margie married and had another child. But tragically, in 1996, she passed away at the age of 26 from cancer. At her funeral, I had the opportunity to talk about all that she had meant in our lives. Our daughter, Margie's birthchild, stood by my side as I spoke. Needless to say, my words were very emotional.

Margie's death was so tragic but, how fortunate that this had been an open adoption. If Jessica's had been a closed adoption, she might never have met Margie, perhaps searching for her later in life only to find that her birthmother had died years before. Even sadder, Margie would have passed away never having known the daughter she had brought into the world nor knowing the good life she had so courageously arranged for her.

No one in the church that day could have missed why openness in adoption is so important.

Earlier, I mentioned a young boy, Jimmy, who asked "Why didn't my mommy even say goodbye?" There is a happy ending to that story. Saddened and hurt by their son's pain, his parents hired a private detective agency to find Jimmy's birthmother. They found her in only three days. Once they contacted her and found that she was agreeable to such a meeting, they arranged for Jimmy to meet her.

❖ It was a remarkable occasion. There was our son, sitting on his birthmother's lap at the local pizza parlor. He was showing her all his scrapbooks and telling her story after story. His birthmother was a nice person and it was obvious to him that he was very important to her. He was overflowing with joy at finally knowing that he had been brought into being with love, not anger. After the initial reunion, Jimmy and his birthmother parted and have only seen each other once or twice in the last few years. But Jimmy is fine now. And so are his parents.

Some form of ongoing contact between birthparents and adopted children is important. That interchange may be on a regular basis (once a year, perhaps, or maybe more frequent) and in person. For some families, the contact is through a birthday card every year. Other times, it is a matter of the birthparents sending a postcard from an interesting place, making an occasional phone call, or getting in touch on special occasions such as a high school graduation. The occasion for a visit may be a special moment in the birthmother's or birthfather's life, such as a new job or a family change.

❖ I can't tell you how much it meant to Lisa, our adopted daughter. There she was being the flower girl at Shane's [her birthmother] wedding. What could be a more powerful statement that although Shane was not Lisa's mother, Lisa was still terribly important to her and both of them to each other.

In the situations where the birthparents do not stay in touch or, for some reason, are not able to do so, the effect is often negative. Adopted children may start to wonder that if their birthparents chose adoption for them out of love and not rejection, why aren't they staying in contact? Why don't they want to know how they are doing in school, with their hobbies, and with their lives in general? Most children would be upset if a favorite uncle or aunt simply dropped out of sight. Whether it's a relative or a birthparent, a child's ability to trust and care can be damaged by feeling abandoned by someone who has been important in his or her life.

When Do Adoptive Parents Tell Their Children that They Are Adopted?

A doptive parents are often anxious about when and how to tell their child about his or her adoption. Should they raise the issue themselves or should they wait until the child asks? How old should the child be before they talk about adoption? How much detail should they provide? One of the delightful aspects of open adoption is that, for many families, this problem simply disappears. The adoption is so much a part of the child's life and family history that there is rarely a need for long explanations. While growing up, the child may ask some limited and specific questions, such as "How come my friends do not have birthmothers?" An older child might ask more sophisticated questions about such matters as the adopting parents' infertility. But these type of inquiries are just questions, not the emotional challenges typical of many closed adoptions. And they can be answered simply, calmly, and frankly.

> ❖ Mark [our adopted son] knew we were trying to adopt another baby. One day he asked me whether the baby was in my tummy yet. I calmly reminded him that his mom could not have babies that way but his birthmother had carried him in her body. Mark thought about that for a minute and then said, "Well, is my new brother or sister in her belly now?" I explained no, we were looking for another birthmother for his sibling. He nodded his head and went back outside with his friends.

The Adopted Child—Peers and Society

What about the adopted child's treatment by friends, relatives, and society in general? In the past, society did not look kindly on an adopted child. Since most babies placed for adoption were the children of unwed mothers, adoption was associated with being an illegitimate child. Even the adopting family itself was seen as less than normal. Since the birthmother was called the "natural mother," the adoptive mother was left as the unnatural parent. Even the practitioners of adoption seemed to share these views with their insistence on such secrecy in the adoption process.

But the social context for an adopted child has changed dramatically in recent years. A child living with his or her nonbiological parents has become commonplace because of the high divorce and remarriage rate. In this more fluid society, the situation of an adopted child no longer seems that unusual.

The very openness of open adoption also affirms the normalcy of a child's being in a family by adoption. In the past, the secrecy imposed on the adoption process reinforced society's negative attitude toward the adopted child. Adopted children often were afraid of being "found out." Open adoption obviously creates a different environment. As we have seen, the adopted child understands that he or she is adopted and knows full well the details surrounding the adoption. As children of open adoption grow up, the people around them —their parents, grandparents, relatives, and friends—discuss the fact of their adoption openly and approvingly. The fear of being suddenly exposed or labeled is virtually nonexistent.

❖ Our daughter, Morgan, is an eleven-year-old adopted through an open adoption. One day, her teacher gave her and the other students in her class an exercise to do about interviewing. They were all to go home and interview their mothers about their labor and delivery and then report the answers to the class. With a closed adoption, such an assignment could have been a disaster for Morgan. All her classmates would have wonderful stories to tell but she would have to say, "I'm adopted and I don't know anything about my birth."

But that is not what happened. When she told me about the assignment, I suggested she call her birthmother on the phone and interview her. Morgan called her. They had not seen each other for about a year, but the connection was still strong. She interviewed her birthmother about her labor and delivery. In the end, Morgan had a great story to tell to her class. All the kids loved it.

In the last few decades, we have witnessed how quickly our society's values and mores can change. This has happened with everything from sex roles to the length of hair, the definition of marriage, work styles, and career paths. For instance, years ago, having a mother who worked full time often implied that a child's family was unusually poor. Today, in most families, both husband and wife work and no one thinks much about it. The same is likely to happen with adoption. By the time most open adoption children enter the school system, the fact of their adoption will seem commonplace.

What about the adopted child's acceptance by the friends and relatives of the adopting parents? Again, the openness of the adoption has major advantages. Nothing about the adoption is hidden away or kept secret. In fact, most prospective adopting couples involve their family and network of friends in the adoption process right from the beginning. They talk to everyone they can about the details of open adoption and their decision to adopt and ask their assistance in spreading the word about their efforts to find a birthparent. Some people are skeptical because they know little about open adoption or share the same stereotypes about birthparents that we discussed earlier. But most adopting parents can explain open adoption to friends and relatives in ways that help to alleviate their fears.

❖ Our family lives far apart and they were very nervous about open adoption at first. But they have become more and more used to the idea because we do have a lot of contact with the birth family. When my mom and sister were out here recently, our son's birthfather, his parents, his sister from L.A., and her son all came over to meet them. My mom was amazed what a nice visit it was and especially how easy it all felt. Everybody is clear he is our son, we are his parents. It was just like cousins or friends visiting.

Open Adoption Does Not Solve Every Problem

Adoptive parents often ask whether open adoption solves all the problems of being an adopted child. The answer is no. In most open adoptions, the child's birthparents do become a part of the adoptive family as relatives. But not all family relationships work out. Perhaps the adopting parents and birthparents will grow apart in their values or ideas and no longer feel comfortable with each other. The same can happen between the adopted children and their birthparents. As the children grow older, they may differ with their birthparents on important matters. In each of these cases, the relationship between the adoptive family and the birthparents can be strained and the relationship eventually broken off.

Nor does open adoption mean all the issues of being adopted disappear for a child. Even with open adoption, even if their birthparents' decision was for the best of reasons, adopted children can still feel rejected. Those feelings can be difficult to handle, especially for teenagers struggling with their identities. Nor does open adoption eliminate all the problems of normal parenting. Adopted children are no better or worse than any other children. The joys and struggles are the same.

❖ As soon as Jane got her driver's license, she came right to me and asked if she could borrow the family car next Saturday. I said "No, I want to be with you when you drive, for the next few weeks anyway." She answered angrily, "Well, I bet my birthmother would have let me use the car!"

But I didn't take the bait. Only the other day, my friend Jack told me he had the same exact argument with his son. Only his son—who is not adopted—said "I bet Jane's dad is nicer than you and lets her use the car."

No one has ever said that parenthood or childhood is easy, and neither is being an adoptive parent or an adopted child. Yet the problems are so much easier to overcome when the child's adoption is open and aboveboard, when the adoption has been a source of pride and caring ever since the parents, birthparents, and child all entered each other's lives.

Who Are the Real Parents?

Will adopted children be confused by having these two sets of parents, adopted and biological? If the children are confused, can the adoptive parents ever feel like true parents, or will they always feel as if they are only sharing parenthood with the birthparents?

How do any of us identify who are our true parents? Is it biology or is it something else altogether? If you ask people what would happen if they suddenly found out that they were adopted, most reply that they would be shocked, hurt, and perhaps furious at their parents for never having told them. But almost everyone admits that this information would not make their parents any less their true mother and father. The secrecy and deception would be the source of their upset more than the actual fact of their adoption. Our parents are our parents not because of egg and sperm, but because, for as long as we can remember, they have always been the people with us and for us as mother and father. The same is true for the children in an open adoption. They know who their parents are: they are people who are committed to them, who are always there, and who love and take care of them as parents.

A clear demonstration of this type of attachment frequently happens at the first visit of the birthparents with the new family. This meeting has a multiple purpose. The birthparents can see for themselves that everything is all right for their child. The adopting parents can show the birthparents how correct they were to choose them to raise their biological child. Whatever the reason for the visit, this still can be a nerve-racking time for the adopting parents. They have just started feeling like a mother and a father. Will the visit of the child's biological parents somehow undermine that wonderful emotion? In reality, the experience is almost always the opposite. The visit confirms for the adoptive parents that they are, indeed, the parents. For the birthparents, seeing their child with its new family deepens their sense that, as one birthmother explained, "the baby is still my baby but she is not my daughter."

❖ We invited Kathy and Mark, the birthparents of our adopted daughter, Georgia, over for their first visit. Georgia was about two months old. We were pretty nervous. We knew Kathy and Mark were not going to change their minds. All their carefully laid plans for each of their lives would be down the drain. And we knew they had chosen us carefully for their daughter. But you never know.

We had Georgia all dressed up and she looked so incredibly cute. In some ways, we wished she did not look that cute—maybe it would be better if she looked more plain to the two of them. But that was not to be. She looked adorable!

After the usual formalities and hellos, I asked Kathy if she would like to hold Georgia. I knew I should offer this to Kathy but it made me nervous. Kathy hesitated. She was just as nervous as I was. She was not really good with babies and this was pretty scary. She seemed reluctant to take the baby, but I think she felt she should. So she said, "Yeah, sure."

Now that I have been the parent of an infant, I realize I should have known exactly what would happen next. Kathy took Georgia and Georgia started to cry. My daughter knew she was not with her mother. My daughter did not need any intellectual analysis of the essence of parenting to know that I was her mother. Kathy and I burst into laughter. Kathy was laughing because she felt so nervous about Georgia's crying. I was laughing the hardest, though. I realized that what I thought would happen—that somehow my little Georgia would scream "Oh my God, you're my birthmother, please take me away"—was pretty ridiculous.

Consistently, both open adoption counselors and adoptive parents find that the children in an open adoption do not feel a contradiction between having one set of regular parents—their adoptive parents—and one set of biological parents. They know exactly who are their parents; the fact that they also have birthparents (and maybe even birthgrandparents) is a plus, not a minus, to these children.

❖ It was our adopted son Carl's sixth birthday and his birthmother, Karen, came for a visit to our home in Iowa. In the first year after Carl's birth, she had seen him every few months, but as time went by, her visits became more of an annual event. But we kept in regular touch with her.

After cake, ice cream, and gifts, the adults were sitting around talking and Carl and the other kids were running around the house. For some reason, the kids started talking about babies. Suddenly, Carl walked over to Karen, his birthmother, pointed to her stomach, and said to the other kids, "That is where I came from." The kids kept on going, but the adults were left speechless. Then a few minutes later, Carl fell down on the stairs and banged his knee. He ran right *past* Karen, without even giving her a look, and straight to me. He was crying loudly "Mommy, Mommy, Mommy." Sure, he knew his biological origins, but he also knew who his mom was.

Not only is the two-parent issue rarely confusing to the adopted child, but it is often a source of joy and support. How could anyone suffer from having too many people in the world who love them?

❖ Our daughter enjoys having so many relatives. To her birthgrandparents and their families, she is just one of the kids when she comes for a visit. She loves all the attention.

❖ As for my son, he knows he has grandparents, god-parents, and birthparents, and that they are all special in their own way. But none of them is ever confused with his real parents—*us*!

❖ We have three adopted children and have become true believers in open adoption, to say the least. For our oldest son, Andrew's, birthday party, we not only invited his regular grandparents (our parents) but his birthgrand-parents as well. And we invited the birthparents and birthgrandparents of both his brother and sister. It was a zoo but great fun. One couple, guests who did not know much about open adoption, asked me if maybe this was too much for Andrew. I had to admit that the party was a little chaotic but I told them they should ask Andrew himself how he felt. When they asked him, he said, "You mean I could have *too many grandparents and too many presents?*" and stalked off shaking his head about how strange adults can be sometimes.

Recently, I watched as a reporter who was writing a story on open adoption interviewed Nick, a seven-year-old boy adopted in an open adoption. The reporter kept asking him if he felt funny about having two sets of parents. Nick kept shaking his head, saying "No," and seemed annoyed with the question. Finally, Nick frowned, shook his head again, and said to the reporter, "You mean to say that I have these par-ents who love me all the time and I have these two other people out there who love me, no matter what, and that is bad? I don't get it!" Then, as if to clinch his argument, Nick stood up and asked the reporter a question: "How many children do you have?" The reporter replied that he had two children, a son and a daughter. Nick looked him right in the eye and asked, "Do *you* find it confusing to have *two* children?" The reporter laughed and finally understood. It was not that Nick had found the perfect analogy but that he had made his point clear. To Nick, having two sets of parents was natural.

Kathleen Silber, co-author of *Children of Open Adoption*,[1] received this letter from a nine-year-old girl about her two sets of parents.

Dear Kathy,

Being adopted is lucky if you think about it.

I think I'm pretty lucky to have two mothers and two fathers.

I really don't think about it much though.

That is all.

Sincerely,
Cara

Open adoption does not mean shared parenthood. Legally, there is only one formal set of parents—the adoptive parents—with the right to make decisions for their child. But the matter goes far beyond legalities. If the birthparents wanted to be parents, they would have kept the child, especially since adoption is so much more difficult than the other alternatives. The birthparents have chosen a particular couple precisely because they wanted this man and woman to be their child's parents. They feel the connection to the child— but as a loving relative, no longer as a parent. And they welcome this feeling with a combination of joy and relief.

❖ Seeing her birthdaughter that first time in our home was an important moment for Kathy [the birthmother], too. She talked later about how she still felt a strong kinship with Olivia. Yet seeing how much she had changed in the months since they had last been together confirmed for her that she was no longer the mother. The feeling was the same for Tim, the birthfather.

❖ The first time I saw my birthson, Max, and I was not the mommy, it was really weird. But to be truthful, I was really glad I wasn't the mommy. He was at that stage where he had just learned to walk and he was going everywhere. Martha [the adopting mother] is just such a good parent and I'm so grateful. I used to think when we were together—Martha and Ken [the adoptive father] and I—that it would be awkward. Would we all compete for Max's attention? But that has never happened. I see how wonderful they are as parents and, in a way, I am learning parenting skills from them for whenever I am ready to be a mother myself.

The adoptive parents' constant interaction with their child quickly drives away any fears they might have about having to share the raising of their new baby.

❖ I used to worry about the birthmother supplanting me as a parent if she came over for visits. But only before I held Tim in my arms. Once I held him, I knew he was my baby and I felt that he knew I was his father. But more than that, I knew that even if his birthmother—whom I like a lot—came over every week or even every day for an hour, nothing could match my being with him all day long, every day, and much of every night as well.

Bonding with an Adopted Child

*M*any adopting parents worry that they will not bond to their adopted child in the same way a biological parent would "naturally" do. In reality, the bond between baby and parent is not biological but mental.[2] Contrary to the common myths about bonding, the process does not always happen instantly for either biological or adoptive parents. More often, bonding occurs over a long period. Some bonding may take place at birth, but for many parents, the profound bond with a child—a bond like no other—develops through a variety of experiences, from seeing the child's first smile to watching their son or daughter graduate from high school or college.

Worries about bonding are almost universal among adoptive parents *before* they have their child and almost equally irrelevant *afterward*. Part of this bonding process is simply constant contact between the newborn baby and the new parents, whether they are related biologically or by adoption. Most adopting parents have a hard time worrying about the abstract question of whether they are the real parents when they have to change diapers ten to twelve times a day, fill baby bottles, and constantly call the doctor with questions about the child. They watch their baby grow, smile, and then laugh for the first time. They feel the infant's vulnerability and dependence on them. Their concern about whether they are entitled to be a parent is overwhelmed by the day-to-day, concrete, immediate experience of being a mother or father. Newly adopted babies have an extraordinary way of reassuring their adoptive mothers and fathers that they are their parents. To put it the other way, they convince them that they are, indeed, their children.

❖ I wondered when I would feel like the real mother instead of thinking that her biological mother was the real one. One morning, when I had changed Lisa's four hundredth diaper, had my fifteenth night in a row of getting woken up, and seen Lisa looking up at me with her first smile—directed at me and me alone, not at her birthmother or birthfather—I knew I was the real mother.

Whether the bonds are instant or grow over time, the ties between adopting parents and adopted children are as strong as any between biological child and biological parent.

❖ There we [the adopting parents] were at the birth. Marti's [the birthmother] sister and I hanging on to each other watching the head of our son-to-be come out. I mean wow, is instantaneous fast enough for the bond to develop?

❖ Our birthmother had him for the first day at the hospital. She had rooming in and I thought, gosh, that is my time to bond. But it didn't matter at all. I mean you get him and you hold him and you feed him and you stare at him. You stare at him for days. You say, oh it's five o'clock, how did the whole day go by just looking at my baby! But this is what we did, we just stared at him and stared at him. There was never any doubt that he was ours.

❖ I can't imagine how I would make her different if I could design her from scratch. A long time ago, I thought that I might find fault with her because she is not my natural child. This was before I saw her. Now I can't see how I could love a child any more than I do Jeanette. The fact of birth or adoption disappears pretty fast once you realize that she is dependent on us to bring her up. Probably I have even more care for Jeanette knowing that I must honor her birthmother's trust in me.

Notes

1. Kathleen Silber and Patricia Martinez Dorner, *Children of Open Adoption* (San Antonio: Corona Publishing Company, 1991).

2. To some extent the emphasis on bonding has been exaggerated. The exaggeration was probably necessary in order to convince the medical world that they should involve mothers and fathers in the birth process. After all, only fifteen or twenty years ago, babies were delivered with the mother under general anesthesia and the father deliberately and totally excluded from the room. With all the stress on the importance of bonding, doctors were persuaded to keep the mother awake and ready to hold the child and, at least in many places, to have the father in the room as well.

8

The Vital Role of Counseling in an Open Adoption

*T*hroughout this book, I have emphasized how extraordinarily rewarding open adoption is for adopting parents, birthparents, and adopted children. At that same time, I've tried to convey that it is also a complicated, emotional, and delicate process. Open adoption, by its very nature, cries out for counseling support. Since closed adoption shrouded over most of the critical issues for adopting parents, birthparents, and adopted children, counseling was almost irrelevant. Open adoption brings these concerns to the forefront, so that they can be addressed and handled, and even become a source of joy instead of pain. But a successful open adoption takes considerable work and care. It requires determination and the commitment to see the process through to the end. And something else is needed: *the best and the most comprehensive counseling support available.*

The need for counseling may seem obvious, yet a surprising number of prospective adopting parents pursue open adoption without this critically needed assistance. Sadly, people hurt by infertility may seek out only the best *short-range* solutions—adoption procedures that seem to get them an infant quickly and easily. Why bother with workshops and counseling sessions, they think, when all they want is a baby?

> ❖ There I was, sitting at my first seminar on adoption. It all sounded good, but also very complicated. I looked around at all the people there. It was not like we had all found out that we were infertile when we were eighteen and signed up for adoption at age twenty. Like myself, everyone there had been through a personal infertility hell—emotion-wise, time-wise, and money-wise. We had all paid our dues. Couldn't they just bring out some babies and hand them out to us instead of making us go through this whole adoption process?

While understandable, such an approach can be tragically shortsighted. Long-term considerations are critical in a process that affects people so profoundly and so deeply influences the rest of their lives. One adopting mother who had seen her adoption nearly fall through because of a lack of just this type of support explained it this way:

> ❖ I don't want to sound crass about it, but when you are buying a house or renting an office, real-estate people always say that there are three crucial criteria: location, location, and location. Well, with adopting a child, there are only three criteria as well: counseling, counseling, and counseling. If the person you are dealing with does not mention counseling in the first sentence, and the second sentence, and the third sentence, and every other sentence from then on, head for the hills.

If adopting parents and birthparents are healthy, caring, even courageous people—as I have maintained throughout this book—why would they need so much counseling help? Counseling does not necessarily mean dealing with deep psychological problems like phobias and psychoses. Many counseling programs today can have a different focus. Their aim is to help men and women deal with specific, critical times in their lives, typically on a short-term basis. The assumption is that the client is mentally healthy but facing an unusually stressful situation. Examples include programs designed to help people make career changes, stop smoking, or reduce work-related stress.

Open adoption counseling takes this latter approach. The counselors do not assume that they are working with people who have emotional problems. In fact, the initial assumption is the opposite. Birthparents, as I have said, tend to be more mature than their peers. Most adopting parents, by virtue of surviving the challenges of trying to conceive a child, have shown their mental fortitude. The counselor's part is not to probe for deep psychological problems but to anticipate and prepare both the adopting parents and birthparents for the concrete problems and issues that usually arise in an open adoption, help them deal with any emotional complications that develop, and, if needed, mediate and resolve any conflicts.

Counseling can play a major role in averting the most obvious tragedy: the birthparents taking their child back after the baby is in the adoptive couple's home. Given the depth and intensity of the emotions involved in an adoption, it is hardly surprising that, without sufficient counseling, many adoptions end this way. Fortunately, *with counseling*, open adoptions rarely fail: counseling-centered open adoption programs typically have a 95 percent or better success rate.

Counseling not only facilitates a successful adoption in the short run but helps lay the groundwork for a healthy adoptive family in the long run. The adoptive parents' experiences at the birth of their child have a profound impact on their lives and their child's. If the birth and adoption process are filled with anger and distrust, the impact can be severe, even if the birthparents do not back out of the adoption. The anguish of that experience can easily spill over to the adopted child and affect the child's delicate and critical opinion about his or her biological origins. In contrast, the positive experiences that characterize an open adoption commonly create the foundation for a stable, happy adoptive family. Besides, adopting parents deserve to have the same joy about the birth of their child as biological parents. When you ask biological parents about their child's birth, they usually talk about their sense of wonder and awe at those moments. Adoptive couples should be able to feel the same way about the birth of their adopted child. Yet, given the delicacy and complications of pregnancy, birth, and delivery, infertility, and adoption, such positive outcomes are not a matter of course. They usually require the support of an experienced and caring counselor throughout the adoption process.

Counseling and the Adoptive Parents

*M*any people assume that the main role of the open adoption counselor is to help the birthparents. In fact, counselors find that their work is as much with the adoptive parents. After all, becoming a parent, even under the best of conditions, is an intense experience. And adoption is not the easiest of undertakings: a certain amount of complication and uncertainty is inherent in even the most secure of adoptions. But there is more. There is the additional stress that results from their past battles with infertility.

For many people, the years of infertility have sapped their energy and made them pessimistic and cynical about ever becoming parents.

❖ Not only did we not look like Ken and Barbie but we did not look like parent material at all. Parents are smiling people with babies, not gloomy people hopelessly giving each other fertility hormone shots and spending half their lives at the hospital having infertility surgery.

Couples often bring these emotions to the adoption process. With adoption, they are once again being asked to risk a considerable amount of time and money. Why should they believe that the adoption path will succeed when other alternatives have not worked? Why would some birthparents, somewhere, ever select them to be the new mother and father of their child? How could they ever trust the birthparents to carry through with their promise to have them adopt their child?

Fortunately, a strong counseling support program can help adoptive parents overcome these concerns. To start with, a counselor guides the couple in working through the general pain of their infertility and restoring their lost self-esteem. Being part of an adoption support group made up of other prospective adopting parents can be instrumental in restoring their energy and enthusiasm. Simply seeing that other people have similar concerns and frustrations is surprisingly comforting.

Adoption is an active process—in contrast to the most typical passivity of medical treatment—that requires considerable energy and resourcefulness. In most open adoption programs, for instance, anywhere from 20 to 40 percent of adopting parents locate their birthparents through contacts with friends and relatives. This requires personal conversations and numerous letters to friends and relatives and friends-of-friends and friends-of-friends-of-friends about their search for a child to adopt. For people with extensive sales backgrounds, this type of outreach might be easy. But other couples find marketing themselves difficult and upsetting, especially if they enter the adoption process feeling disheartened by their infertility. A competent counselor can help the couple see that they are not selling some sleazy product but reaching out to their family and friends about something special: their desire to be a loving mother and father.

Eventually, most prospective adopting parents are contacted about a particular set of birthparents. How do they then decide whether to work with these young people? For most people, these are the first birthparents they have encountered. Besides, the adoption process is often so emotion-laden that being objective is difficult. Here the counselor, as a caring yet impartial intermediary, has an important role to play. At the match meeting, the counselor poses the difficult questions that everyone else may be too hesitant or too embarrassed to ask.

> ❖ Though we had been with the birthparents all weekend, we were just too shaky to ask many questions. When the match started, though, Gail, our counselor, just started asking the questions and it all seemed natural. We were relieved that she was asking them and that we were getting answers.

Afterwards, counselors help both the adopting parents and birthparents decide if the matchup is right for them. They can provide the adopting parents with an assessment of the potential success of the adoption based on their professional experience with similar situations.

Sometimes the adopting parents and birthparents are mismatched. When that happens, saying "no" is not easy for anyone. Given how anxious prospective adopting parents are about finding a baby, turning down any opportunity is not easy, no matter how unsuitable. A counselor can support the adopting parents in making the decision they need to make, even if the consequences seem dire at the time. They need reassurance from the counselor that they will have other opportunities to adopt.

Once a suitable match is found, the counselor provides ongoing support for the adoptive parents as well as mediation in case of any misunderstandings between them and the birth-parents. Though a strong tie often develops between adopting parents and birthparents, even in the best of adoptions, this bond is a delicate one. For instance, although there are usually major differences in age and experience between the adoptive parents and birthparents, adoptions work best when everyone feels like peers and equals. No one likes to feel at a disadvan-tage in a relationship, and young people find it especially galling. If the connection between adoptive parents and birth-parents starts to feel like the old stereotype of a well-heeled, settled couple matched with a poor waif of a birthmother, problems are likely to develop. This issue sometimes arises in relation to medical testing for the birthmother. Her phy-sician may request certain tests to check on everything from rubella (German measles) to HIV infection. Since the birth-mothers are committed to having healthy children, they are willing and anxious to take these tests. In some cases, though, requesting these procedures can be a touchy issue. For in-stance, in theory, asking the birthparents to have an AIDS/HIV test should not be seen as questioning their moral stand-ing. In reality, however, many people take it that way. Many birthmothers are already ill at ease about being younger and less established than the adopting parents. Insisting on this test may make them feel worse and undermine the trust that has been developing between the adopting parents and birth-parents. To avoid this, the counselor can recommend that both the adopting parents and birthparents take the test. Though not technically necessary for the adopting parents, the test does no harm—it is painless and inexpensive—and plenty of good, preserving the feelings of mutual respect be-tween adoptive parents and birthparents.

Another typical scenario finds the adopting parents starting to panic a few weeks before their birthmother's due date. Their friends have given them a baby shower, they have fixed up the nursery, and they have made plans for one or both of them to take a leave of absence from work. Suddenly, they realize that their entire future lives, their only chance of ever becoming parents, is solely in the hands of a young woman (and man) whom they have met only in the last few months. This can be a terrifying prospect. If no counseling is available, the couple may start calling their birthmother every day and asking her to reassure them that she is not going to change her mind. Typically, the first few times they ask, she has no hesitation about answering their question in the affirmative. But as the requests for reassurance multiply, the birthmother may start to feel that the adopting parents do not trust her, that they are not taking her plans for her life seriously nor her concerns for her child. She may become increasingly frustrated and even angry with them. Sadly, the couple's fears about their adoption may soon turn into a self-fulfilling prophecy as the birthmother starts searching for a way out.

Fortunately, that type of tragedy can be avoided. The adopting parents' worries and concerns in this type of situation are not surprising, abnormal, or unethical. The problem comes only when they try to get the birthmother to provide them with constant reassurance. They are asking her, in effect, to become their counselor just when her hands are full dealing with her own emotions. What makes more sense is for the adopting parents to seek support and assistance from a counselor or, perhaps, from fellow members of an adoption support group, not from the birthmother. In this way, they can be assured that their last minute jitters are normal and to be expected. They can get the support they need without undermining their positive connection with the birthparents.

A counselor can also help the adopting parents and birthparents plan ahead about some of the important details in their relationship. A number of delicate issues are likely to arise over the years, and coming to an agreement about them in advance is helpful. For instance, should the adopting couple be in the delivery room during the birth? How long should the baby remain in the hospital? How frequently should the birthparents visit in the months after the birth and during the years of the child's life? Who should call first to arrange these visits? Some of these issues seem small, some major, but a counselor encourages all participants to think about what they will want at those times and come to some agreement with each other about how these situations will be handled.

In many adoptions, the birthfather plays only a small role or none at all. Nevertheless, a counselor can reach out to these young men to help them deal with their own unique fears and concerns. Many birthfathers are reluctant to become involved in their child's adoption out of fear of the unknown. Some are angry with the birthmother for ending their relationship and refusing to mother their child. But a patient, nonconfrontational approach often succeeds in getting the birthfather more involved. The effort is almost always worthwhile. Having the birthfather's support is far better than enduring his opposition, and he deserves the opportunity to be engaged in the adoption of his own child. Moreover, information about him is an important part of the adopted child's heritage.

❖ The birth father was a really important issue for us. For our daughter's sake, it was worth all the counseling we arranged for him in order to get to meet him and not just have information on him on paper. Even if we do lose contact with him in the future, we have been with him enough so we can tell her what he was like.

The situation is similar with birthgrandparents, the parents of the birthmother and birthfather. They, too, usually merit involvement in the adoption process and appreciation for their feelings of loss and grief. In the absence of some type of support and understanding, birthgrandparents may become angry and bitter and even try to block the adoption. Here again, a patient but persistent counselor can play an effective role in addressing the needs of these people who are so important not only to the adoption but to the birthparents and the birthchild.

Because emotions run high at the birth, a counselor plays a critical role at this time. The most effective counselor is one who not only has experience with open adoption but also understands the special dynamics of hospital settings and is familiar with the hospital's procedures and regulations.

There are also important counseling concerns after the adoption has been completed, particularly if the relationship between the adoptive parents and birthparents has encountered any problems. Even if the connection has been close, misunderstandings can still arise. In such cases, the adoptive family may call on the counselors who have been involved in their adoption since the beginning.

❖ Our relationship with our birthmother has recently gotten much better. A turning point came a couple of weeks ago when we met with Kelly and the counselor who handled our adoption. She helped us work through some things that were keeping us from having a close relationship. She [the birthmother] got to tell us all her deep worries about us and we told her what concerned us. That all seemed to help a lot. She clearly wants to have a continuing relationship with us and we want that as well.

Whether or not counseling is provided during the adoption process, those adoptive parents whose adoptions fail often benefit from counseling support. Counseling assists the adoptive parents through the necessary grieving process about the lost child and, at the same time, helps them rebuild their hopes and strengths for another attempt to adopt.

❖ After our adoption collapsed, we thought we should give up: we just could not go through that again. We met with our counselor and she reassured us that our grief about losing our opportunity was normal but that we needed to find a way out of that pain. We needed to get back on the road to becoming parents. We started to look for a child again.

Counseling Support for the Birthparents

A major focus of any open adoption counseling program is the birthparents. Pregnancy is an intense experience for almost anyone: physically, hormonally, and emotionally. Not surprisingly, most birthparents, even those most certain of their decisions, are disturbed by feelings of doubt and loss about having their babies adopted. A counselor can play an important role in providing them support for their adoption decision and helping them understand and get through the pain and grief that accompanies it. A well-designed counseling program helps the birthparents explore their past life, their plans for the future, and their motivations for making their decisions. Often the most important function of the counselor is far less fancy. They are there as a friend to the birthparent, a friend who understands both the birthparents' courage and their hurt.

> ❖ My family was involved with me in the adoption but they really didn't understand how I felt. Their support was just not the same as what Gail and Eileen [the open adoption counselors], and especially the other birthmothers in our support group, could give me. They really let me see that I was making the right decision.

A close connection between counselor and birthmother or birthfather can turn out to be critical. For instance, even in the best of adoptions, it is not unusual for a birthmother, a few weeks before the baby is due, suddenly to have doubts about whether she has picked the best couple to raise her child. Given the finality and magnitude of her decision, such last minute questions are not surprising or abnormal. If she does nothing about these feelings, the adoption may soon be in doubt. She is unlikely to discuss her doubts with the attorney handling the adoption for fear that he or she will threaten her with some type of legal action. She could talk to the adopting couple about her concerns, but they would have to have the patience of a saint to listen calmly to her recitation of what she does not like about them. What a birthmother usually needs most at that point is to talk with a trusted counselor. Her counselor reassures her that these doubts are normal and helps her remember why she chose this particular couple in the first place.

For many birthmothers, the most difficult moments come a few weeks after the birth of their children. With the help of the adopted parents and their own friends and family, they may have been able to get through the birth itself. But a few weeks later, the baby is gone, hormones are running amok, and the lifelong impact of the decision starts to come home. The birthmother experiences a deep sense of loss and grief. Most people feel that depth of pain only with the death of a relative or friend. But in those situations, there is nothing they can do to bring the deceased person back to life. In an adoption, in contrast, the birthmother *can* bring the lost person back. She can ask that her child be returned. Most reclaims—where the birthmother changes her mind and wants the baby back—occur at this point if the birthmother (and even the birthfather) does not have access to an experienced counselor to help with an intense sense of loss.

When this grief and pain hit, most birthparents feel too vulnerable and scared to call for help except for someone with whom they have already developed a close and trusting relationship. They are unlikely to call an attorney since that relationship is usually so formal, or even a counselor with whom they have had only limited contact. Here, in particular, the importance of establishing a close and continuing connection between counselor and birthparent early in the adoption process becomes apparent.

❖ Though counseling was strongly recommended, Leslie [our birthmother] felt she didn't need it. She knew what to do and she was feeling right about it. Her attorney felt that she had a family support system and that she was clear about her decision. So Sean and I accepted Leslie's decision. That was a terrible mistake.

Soon after the baby was born, Leslie asked for the child back. We cared for her, we understood how she felt, but we were heartbroken. I believe that an established relationship with a counselor could have provided Leslie with the added strength that a birthmother needs to survive during this very emotional experience. A preestablished relationship can build a trust that is essential during the period of crisis. We had been encouraged to pursue Leslie's counseling needs, but we were naive and underestimated the importance of this service. No matter how strong or logical the birthmother is during that hour of giving birth, she needs professional support.

What Are the Roles of Lawyers and Doctors in Open Adoption?

*I*f counseling support is so vital in an open adoption, then what part should be played by physicians and attorneys? There is clearly a place for competent lawyers in an open adoption. This is particularly true in an independent or private adoption where the laws can be extremely complicated. There is also a need for doctors to guide the birthmother's prenatal care and assist in the birth of the child. Yet, though legal and medical issues are important, they are generally less critical than emotional concerns in an adoption. For that reason, we would expect that counseling support programs would play the primary role in most open adoptions. For reasons unique to modern adoption, that is not always the case. In fact, many people choose to have a lawyer or doctor as their chief source of help in their adoptions.

Why have doctors and attorneys become so important in adoption? Years ago, almost all formal adoptions were handled by adoption agencies, staffed by counselors who guided birthparents through the adoption process. In the last two decades, all that has changed dramatically. Because so many conventional agencies refused to open their adoptions, birthparents soon went elsewhere, and so did prospective adopting parents. With traditional agencies forfeiting their central role in adoptions, somebody needed to step in, and doctors and lawyers had at least some familiarity with the process. Today, most adoptions of healthy infants are handled outside regular adoption agencies, often by attorneys and doctors who once played only minor roles.

It is easy to see why doctors were a reasonable substitute for adoption agencies. After all, pregnant women came to them first, and doctors were not restricted by the laws that governed conventional agencies. They could be more flexible in their approach to adoption. By the 1960s, many adoptions were being facilitated by physicians. The involvement of doctors in adoption, though, has been limited. Most physicians are busy enough handling medical issues without adding a large number of adoptions to their workload.

For the legal profession, on the other hand, an increase in attorney involvement in adoption offered many advantages. The number of attorneys has increased significantly in recent years and the pressure to develop new types of law practices has grown. For many lawyers, handling an adoption is also a more positive experience than the more strident civil or criminal cases that most atttorneys undertake. This more benevolent quality of adoption law has been particularly appealing to the increasing number of women in the legal profession.

As more attorneys started to practice adoption law, they

realized they could offer some important advantages over conventional agencies. In many states, they were not subject to the limiting procedures required of licensed agencies. Most attorneys were not familiar with the traditional social work approach to adoption and, consequently, were not bogged down in the ideology of secrecy and shame so common to adoption agencies. In fact, many attorneys felt no reluctance in openly seeking out birthparents for their clients. If being more open or treating the birthmothers with more "TLC" than conventional agencies would help, they would gladly do it. As a result, attorneys started attracting an increasing number of birthparents and, as a consequence, a large number of prospective adopting parents.

For prospective adopting parents, there is a certain appeal in having an adoption handled exclusively through an attorney. Using an attorney can be expensive but all that seems required is filling in a few papers and paying the legal bills. There are no workshops, counseling concerns, or extended relationships with birthparents. But there can be serious problems. All too often, attorneys ignore the important role of counseling in an open adoption and emphasize a purely legalistic approach. Yet at the heart of most adoptions are not legal issues but a complex of emotional concerns. When and if the attorney emphasizes the critical role of counseling, a close partnership between counselor and attorney can be fruitful for everyone involved in the adoption. The problem is that many adoption lawyers insist that legal issues are primary and, as a result, the vital counseling needs of the adoptive parents and birthparents are not addressed.

Part of the problem with adoptions handled solely by attorneys stems from the very traditions of the legal profession. Attorneys are almost universally taught to view the situation of their clients as adversarial. It is one side against the other, their clients versus a person, company, or government bureaucracy that is injuring or threatening them. While an attorney can be an invaluable advocate in battle or hard-fought negotiations, such an adversarial approach is not only inappropriate in an adoption but can be the cause of considerable harm. Seeing an adoption in adversarial terms—the adoptive parents versus the birthparents—is a fundamental misunderstanding of the nature of the open adoption process. Certainly there can be disagreements, misunderstandings, and tensions in an open adoption. Yet the process still works best if all parties see the adoption not as a power struggle between the adoptive parents and birthparents but as a mutually beneficial process for everyone. The adopting parents are grateful to the birthparents for allowing them to have the joy of becoming parents. The birthparents are thankful to the adopting parents for giving them the opportunity to go on with their lives and yet know that their child has a wonderful home. This sense of sharing and mutual enrichment is central to the open adoption process. When adopting parents and birthparents view each other as opponents, the adoption typically either fails or turns into a bitter experience for everyone.

As an example of the problem with the adversarial approach, consider the advice many attorneys give prospective adopting parents about the letter they are to write to potential birthparents. As a matter of course, this letter includes a photograph of the prospective adopting parents. If the couple has a child already, many attorneys will recommend that he or she *not* appear in the picture. Since some birthmothers prefer couples without any previous children, the lawyers reason, leaving out the couple's child will give their clients a competitive edge. As an adversarial strategy, this may be useful advice. But what happens when they all meet and the birthparents realize they have been misled? With such a poor beginning, what chance will the adopting couple have to build the trusting relationship with the birthparents that is so important to a successful open adoption?

❖ Jim and Bonnie had four adopted children, mostly through foster adoption. When they approached a well-known attorney, an adoptive father himself, he suggested that they use a photo that included only the two of them, not their children.

Jim looked at the attorney, nodded to Bonnie, and they walked out. They were proud of their wonderful family. There was no way in the world that they were going to hide them.

Another possible problem with the strictly legalistic approach arises from the way many lawyers handle the issue of birthfather's rights. Some attorneys will hint or recommend to the birthmother that it might be to her advantage if she claims that she does not know the identity of the birthfather or that she was sexually assaulted. In the short-run, this can speed up the adoption process considerably since, in such cases, the birthfather's rights can be quickly terminated. In the long run, though, this leaves the adopted child with no information about his or her biological father. As with the secrecy of older forms of closed adoption, this can have serious consequences for the child, who wonders why information about his or her birthfather is withheld.

❖ My attorney suggested that we hint to Marsha, our birthmother, that she tell the social workers that she did not know who the birthfather was, or maybe even that she was raped. He said it would simplify the paperwork immensely. It sounded good to us. Less paperwork sounded great, and who wanted to deal with the birth-father anyway? And Marsha was so mad at the guy, she probably would agree to do it.

Then I thought, wait a minute. If Marsha is willing to stretch the truth about the birthfather, maybe she is stretching the truth in other things. Or, the other way. Maybe if we are willing to go along with her stretching the truth, she will think we are the ones who cannot be trusted.

And then it really hit me. What happens when my

child asks about his birthparents? I can tell him that Marsha was terrific and chose us to be his parents out of love. But what if we are asked about the birthfather? Will I tell my child that his or her birthfather was a rapist or an "unknown"?

I called my lawyer and told him, "No thanks!"

Choosing Between an Independent Practitioner or a Licensed Agency

*H*ow can prospective adopting parents choose between licensed adoption agencies vs. private adoption practitioners, either counselors in private practice or attorneys? In some states, there is little choice: only agency adoptions are permitted. In other situations, private adoption may be the only alternative because there are no agencies in the state providing open adoptions. If there is a choice, both approaches have advantages and disadvantages.

In a *licensed agency* adoption, the state specifically grants the organization, usually a nonprofit institution, the power to process adoptions in return for the agency adhering to specific state regulations. The birthparents "relinquish" or "surrender" their child to the agency and the child is then "placed" with the adoptive parents. Under most state laws, once the birthparents have signed these forms, there is almost no way for them to revoke their agreement to the adoption. Most agencies work only with clients in their own locality but there are a few nationwide adoption programs.

Most agencies are staffed by social workers and mental health professionals. This is critical given the vital role of counseling in open adoptions. The requirement that the agencies meet state licensing standards for adoption is also reassuring. Though the agency home study process can be trying for adoptive parents, many birthparents prefer choosing adopting parents for their child who have been approved through this process.

In the past, most licensed agencies followed *closed* adoption procedures. Today, these programs are moving toward openness in adoption but the change is not easy. Going from open to closed adoption is not simply a matter of learning new counseling techniques but requires a fundamental shift in ideology and attitude. Open adoption mandates that the social workers turn over their traditional control over the adoption process to the individual birthparents and adopting parents. Many agencies have a hard time making this change and finding a local agency genuinely committed to fully open adoption may be difficult. Hopefully, the listing of open adoption programs in the Appendix will help.

Open adoption agencies offer another important advantage. In traditional adoption, a strict set of criteria was used to decide which couples could adopt. In contrast, most open adoption agencies are careful to provide birthparents with as wide a range of choice of adoptive parents as possible. To do so, they have eliminated most of those past barriers to being approved for adoption such as age (over 35 or 40 years old), religion, length of marriage, church attendance, or marital history (i.e., the number of previous marriages). Most agencies no longer, as they did in the past, refuse to work with adoptive parents who already have an adopted or biological child. Of course, any evidence of drug use or abusive behavior by the prospective adopting parents is still grounds for rejection.

Unfortunately, some prospective adopting parents may not be able to find any agencies in their state that do not have these arbitrary rules and exclusions.

❖ I did not have to ask anyone for permission to marry my husband. Nor did anyone do a home study on me to see if

I would be a suitable wife. Why does the state feel they have the right to control my life just because I cannot have a child by no fault of my own?

In a *private* adoption, the practitioners or attorneys are not specifically licensed by the state to handle adoptions. The state allows them to do so, however, if they follow specific state laws covering private adoption. There are important differences in how adoptions are finalized in agency adoption versus private adoption. Since agencies are officially licensed, they are "arms of the law" and have considerable power over the adoption process. In contrast, since there is no state certification process for private adoption, finalizing private adoptions is more strictly controlled and the birthparents have greater leeway in their decision. The birthparents usually have a considerable amount of time (sometimes up to six months or more) to change their minds about the adoption of their child. This can be very trying, to say the least, for the newly adoptive parents.

In terms of private adoption, most have the advantage of being relatively new; they do not need to overcome a past tradition of closed adoption. In those states, where many agencies still have restrictions on who can adopt, a private adoption may be the only alternative. Every state requires some type of investigation and home study before a private adoption is finalized. Often, though, the process in a private adoption is less detailed than the home study conducted in agency adoptions.

In private adoptions, the birthparents have the legal right to choose the adopting parents themselves. In reality, these decisions are often made by the attorney or doctor handling the case. Other private adoption programs do provide counseling but vary widely in the breadth and depth of the educational, support, advising, and counseling services that they offer. Sometimes, the counseling staff is small, inexperienced or only available on a volunteer basis. Because private and attorney adoption programs are unregulated, both adopting parents and birthparents have a harder time verifying the legitimacy of any one program.

Perhaps the greatest problem with private adoption is their lack of counseling support. Most private adoptions are handled by adoption law firms or doctor's offices with little or no provision for comprehensive counseling before, during, or after the birth. In some cases, no counseling is provided at all. In other situations, counseling is available but it is limited in extent and duration and seen as only secondary to the legal process.

The choice of adoption programs is important and there are key questions to ask that may help guide your decision:

1. What are the program's restrictions regarding age, children in the home already, religion, etc.

2. Are the counseling staff counseling professionals? What is the screening process for birthparents? Is counseling offered both to the birthparents and the adoptive parents? Are the counselors experienced with open adoption or only with general counseling issues? Is counseling also available to the birthfather and the birthgrandparents? What type of ongoing support and follow-up is included in the program?

3. Are there educational programs to help adoptive parents understand openness in adoption?

4. Do the fees cover all the services needed or are many services, particularly advertising and outreach, only available at an additional cost. What happens if the first adoption attempt falls through; do you have to start paying all over?

5. How does the program find birthparents? Do they have advertising and community outreach programs or do they consider this unprofessional? Do they have an extensive referral network with social service and medical professionals? If the facilitator is an attorney, are health and counseling programs in the area willing to refer to private attorneys or do they prefer recommending nonprofit, licensed organizations?

6. Who plays the critical role in deciding who adopts what child: the state, the attorney, the agency, or the birthparents and adoptive parents? Are the birthparents only shown 'selected' prospective adopting parents or all possibilities? If there is a selection process, how does this work?

7. Does the program help negotiate an agreement between the adoptive parents and birthparents about post-birth contact?

8. Are newly born infants placed with the adoptive parents at birth or are they placed first in foster homes?

9. How quickly can adoptions be finalized? How often do the birthparents ask for their child back after the birth?

10. Since adoption is a lifetime experience, what post-adoption programs are offered?

11. What is the reputation of the program in the community? Can they provide the name of 'satisfied' adoptive couples?

Choosing Between Semi-Open and Fully Open Adoption

Since open adoption is relatively new, there is no single, universally agreed on, standard for what constitutes an open adoption. There are moves in this direction, through, for instance, the certification program of the National Federation for Open Adoption Education.

Nevertheless, there are some fairly clear differences among open adoption programs. Some adoption organizations considered their procedures *fully* open adoption. This usually means that the important decisions in the adoption – such as who will adopt which child – are left strictly up to the adoptive parents and birthparents. Moreover, there is usually no restriction on either the adoptive parents' or birthparents' use of names, exchange of information, or maintaining ongoing contact. In contrast, in what is often called *semi-open* adoption, there are usually limitations imposed on the decision-making power of all the parties, on the sharing of information, and on contact before and after birth.

How can prospective adopting parents decide whether to pursue fully open or semi-open adoption? Is insisting on fully open adoption too extreme or too rigid because this process involves such a variety of people and such complex human emotions? Since open adoption is somewhat new, would it be better to start with the more limited forms of openness offered by semi-open adoption programs? Then birthmothers could choose the parents for their child but only after their possible choices have been narrowed and screened by a professional counselor. Adopting parents and birthparents could meet each other face-to-face but only exchange first names. They would make a commitment to stay in touch with each other but only through an intermediary.

The moderation of such programs is appealing. Yet on closer examination, the seemingly reasonable compromises of semi-open adoption can often bring adoptive parents some of the worst headaches associated with closed adoption and few of the more important benefits of open adoption.

At the heart of the open adoption are two basic beliefs: one, that adoptions work best for everyone (including the adopted child) if the procedures that are followed assume that both adoptive parents and birthparents are healthy people, not unhealthy, and, two, that everyone involved in the adoption is deserving and capable of making the critical decisions needed. Birthparents in particular, but adoptive parents as well, feel more comfortable when they, not others, are making the decisions that will so deeply affect their lives. This happens when the birthparents choose the new adoptive parents from among *all* the people working with the program without restriction or limitation. The same applies to the adoptive parents' choice of birthparents. The sense of respect and cooperation that is then generated carries over to the relationship between the adoptive parents and birthparents and is one of the reasons why those connections so often flower and bloom. Moreover, treating the adoption process as an arduous yet positive experience lays the groundwork for the adopted child to see the adoption as equally healthy and positive. In addition, the complete involvement of all parties in all critical decisions assures each that no one has been tricked, pressured, or cajoled during the adoption process. This approach helps ensure that neither adoptive parents nor birthparents will want to change those decisions later on.

The semi-open adoption approach can seriously undermine these benefits. If the birthparents are only allowed to choose from *some* of the agency's prospective adopting parents, there is an implication that they do not know what is best even for their own children. At worst, some birthparents find this offensive and abandon the adoption altogether. At best, some birthparents can accept these restrictions but feel that a negative and demeaning tone has been established for the adoption.

Moreover, how does the agency or private practitioner select which prospective adopting parents are to be shown to which birthparents? It would be one thing if there were universal agreement on how to predict who will be the best parents for a child. But there is not, except on obvious matters ruling out child abusers or drug addicts. For instance, some people insist that parents should be relatively young while others argue that being older and settled is more important. Having considerable financial resources is seen as central by some, as irrelevant by others. Some observers believe that a previous divorce is a sign of emotional instability. Others maintain that this may show a praiseworthy determination to find the right lifetime partner. The issue is not that age, financial stability, marital history, or any other factor is never important. The problem is that this is a personal and subjective decision. Certainly prospective adopting parents may want to involve a counselor to help them decide if they are ready to become parents. Equally, people with a record of serious mental, criminal, or drug problems should probably not be accepted. But beyond those considerations, an agency's insistence that only their staff can decide who is ready to be parents may establish the same demeaning and negative tone for the adoptive parents as restricting the choices of new parents does for the birthparents.

This same argument holds true for the limitation of exchanging only first names that is common to many semi-open adoption programs. This may sound reasonable, but it too masks disrespect for everyone—as if the parties involved in the adoption are criminals or spies in some clandestine national security operation. This arbitrary rule is particularly awkward in light of the intimate discussions that take place, even in semi-open adoption between adopting parents and birthparents. In the context of revealing details about each other's private lives, hopes, and dreams, maintaining secrecy about their full names seems ludicrous.

Many semi-open adoption programs also insist that any contact between adopting parents and birthparents after the birth of the adopted child be limited to letters and photos exchanged strictly through the agency. The message of such restrictions is once again that adopting parents and birthparents cannot be trusted to talk to each other.

Most of the limitations imposed in open adoption are intended to protect the adoptive parents. But they often have the opposite effect. Keeping the adoptive parents and birthparents apart from each other prevents the development of the close bond and sense of mutual trust that is essential to a successful open adoption.

Semi-open adoption programs are important steps in the right direction away from the problems and pains of closed adoption. In some communities, they are the best that is available. This may well change as soon as awareness increases of the unnecessary hurt and pain that can come from the restrictions imposed by these forms of open adoption.

Dear Roy and Lynette,

There is something that has been bothering me lately. I wanted to tell you exactly how I felt the day that I chose you to be Ann's adoptive parents. My caseworker gave me three sets of profile letters. Yours was the first one that I read. Even before I had finished reading all three of the sets, it was already clear to me that the two of you were going to be the proud parents of a wonderful baby girl.

From that day on, I wanted to call you to tell you our good news. We were going to have a baby! I wanted you to feel the same excitement and anticipation that I was feeling. I thought that would be wonderful for all of us.

I wanted so badly for you to be there when our baby was born. In my heart, I felt that this was your baby, too. You should have the joy of experiencing every stage of her life—including her birth.

I wanted so badly to be there when you chose her name. I wanted to know what kind of place she would be growing up in. I wanted to know your family. I wanted to be the one to call you (since I knew that you wouldn't be there) when you became mommy and daddy. But, most of all, I wanted to become your friend.

There are so many things that I couldn't do or have because the Mission Home was trying to protect you . . . but what were they trying to protect you from? Were they trying to protect you from the risk of experiencing even a fraction of the pain that I would feel when I released my child into your home and hearts? Were they trying to protect you from me—the one who already loved you and trusted you enough to take this wonderful child to raise and love as your very own? I still don't understand. I probably never will.

I hope that you can understand where these feelings

have come from. They have lived inside of me for a long time. I finally realize that I need to be honest with you and with myself before I can truly be happy and before you will ever be able to understand my needs.

I love you all. Kiss and hug Ann for me. Tell her how much I love her. I hope to hear from you soon.

Love,
Melinda

Notes

1. The National Federation for Open Adoption Education can be contacted at 391 Taylor Boulevard, Suite 100, Pleasant Hill, CA 94523, (510) 827-2229.

9

The Joys of Parenthood

A final note. The infertility process can be so grueling that people start to lose sight of why they were determined to have a child in the first place. To start with, there are the friends and relatives who make annoying comments about "relaxing" and drinking wine or taking a vacation to solve the problem. Then there are the people who tell you that becoming a parent is not that important anyway. They bemoan how a new baby means endless nights without sleep, no more movies, concerts, or dinners out, and endless diapers and hassles with baby-sitters. Friends with teenage children may even add, "If you really want a kid that badly, just take one of mine." And there are always situations that seem to confirm how hard it can be to be a parent.

❖ What I hate the most about infertility treatment is getting up at seven o'clock in the morning, making love to my wife though we can barely talk to each other, and getting to the doctor by eight. To make this easier on us, we usually go out to dinner the night before so we can be a little friendlier. Without fail, though, there is a little kid at the next table throwing food and making a big mess. We start thinking, "Why are we going to all this trouble to get one of those?"

Under this type of pressure, many people get discouraged not only about their infertility but about parenthood itself. Yet without a clear eye on the prize—becoming a mother or father—pursuing the medical or adoption path can be too overwhelming.

So how important is the goal of being a parent? Is being a mother or father that rewarding? The answer, for most people, is that parenting is an experience of exceptional joy. Yes, it is a great deal of work. But what goals worth attaining are not? Yes, people do miss seeing movies during the early years of their child's life. But there are VCRs and videotapes. In spite of all the horror stories about taking care of a new baby, there are no known deaths from getting too little sleep or touching baby poop. But there is more, much more.

Most couples underestimated the myriad rewards of being a mother or father. There is the special way a child can love a parent that simply cannot be matched by any other experience.

❖ I have known for years that I am a good public speaker. The other day, though, my six-year-old daughter came in at the end of my speech. The talk over, I walked back to give her a hug. She looked up at me and said with such pride, "Daddy, I didn't know you were a teacher." Nothing, Nobel Prize, Pulitzer Prize, Academy Award, a million dollars, could have touched me more deeply.

Most parents find that the most powerful part of parenting is not how deeply their children love them, but how extraordinary it feels to love their child. Outside of parenting, few people experience the absolute, unconditional, and overwhelming quality of the love they feel for a son or daughter. There is a purity and joy in the love of a child that is fundamentally different from other forms of love.

Parenthood also provides a profound renewal of faith in the human race. Someone once asked Simon Wiesenthal, the great documenter of the Holocaust, how he could bring children into the world having seen how horrible human beings can be to each other. He replied that without children we would lose our most important connection to the wonder of human life. He was right. There are few things more amazing than watching a child go from being able only to cry, eat, and soil diapers to learning to walk and talk and read. When a child struggles to do things we take for granted—such as speaking the complicated and irrational language we call English, or any other language for that matter—it seems like a miracle that such a tiny thing can do so at all. But the miracle does happen. And though millions of children have done it before, when it is your own child, it is still thrilling.

The joy of parenting often surprises men the most. Women generally grow up planning to be mothers and expecting it to be a wonderful experience. Most men have more limited expectations. They think it will be nice to be a dad, play with their kids, and be proud of their sons or daughters. But they are not sure if it will be much more than that. Then they find themselves with their new baby and are completely entranced.

❖ Marty has been "Mr. 60 hours a week" and totally committed to his job. But when Mikey [his adopted son] came along, things changed. Marty used to go in at 6:00 or 7:00 every morning; now it's about 8:30 or later. Sometimes I catch him sitting there with our infant son, talking to him as if there's nobody else around: "We're going to do this and we're going to do that . . ." It's just great.

❖ A ninety-three-year-old lady came up to me as I was thumbing through six-month-size clothes and said, "What are you doing here—are you a father?" I said, "Yes," and told her that we were adopting a little boy. She looked at me again and said, "My god, I have not seen many men out buying baby clothes, at least not as excited as you look." There I was, holding stuff up and having a good time. Now sometimes I get up with him at 3:30 in the morning. My eyes feel like they are hanging out of my cheeks, but there he is smiling and I would not miss a moment.

No matter how great their initial fantasy about what it will be like to be a parent, people are rarely disappointed.

❖ Before our first adoption, I used to wonder if spending all this time and money on infertility and then adoption was going to be worth it. Maybe we should save all that and just enjoy each other. Now that I am about to adopt my second child, everything looks different. I don't care how much time it takes, how much money it costs. I will sell the car, sell the house, quit my job, and start all over if I have to. Whenever I have any doubts about that, I just think of any one special moment with my son—a smile, the first word, a million things—and all hesitation is gone instantly.

Appendix: Open Adoption Centers

The following listing includes adoption organizations in the United States and Canada that are certified as having open adoption practitioners on their staff. All are members of the National Federation for Open Adoption Education.

ARIZONA

Arizona Children's Home Association
P.O. Box 7277
Tucson, AZ 85725
602-222-7611
800-947-7611

Christian Family Care Agency
12720 E. Chukut Tr.
Tucson, AZ 85749
602-749-1513

Christian Family Care Agency
1121 E. Missouri
Phoenix, AZ 85014
602-234-1935

Southwest Adoption Center
225 N. Jacs Place
Tucson, AZ 85748
602-722-0380

CALIFORNIA

Adoption Network
5468 Pire Avenue
San Diego, CA 92122
619-453-9833

Nanette Kuhre
1655 Balboa Court
Pleasant Hill, CA 94523
510-689-2171

Family Growth Center
1558 Grissom Street
Thousand Oaks, CA 91362
805-341-6422

Family Service of Los Angeles
23101 Middlebank Drive
Newhall, CA 91321
805-259-8518

Independent Adoption Center
8616 La Tijera Blvd., Suite 208
Los Angeles, CA 90045
310-215-3180

Independent Adoption Center
2500 Zanella Way, Suite A
Chico, CA 95928
916-893-0403

Independent Adoption Center
391 Taylor Blvd., Suite 100
Pleasant Hill, CA 94523
510-827-2229

Planned Parenthood of Santa
Cruz County
90 Mariposa Avenue
Watsonville, CA 95076
408-724-7525

Sutter Hospital/Birth Connection
5708 Thames Way
Carmichael, California 95608
916-485-4937

The Birth Connection
P.O. Box 277434
Sacramento, CA 95827
916-451-9868

FLORIDA

The Adoption Centre, Inc.
500 N. Maitland Ave., Suite 305
Maitland, FL 32751
407-740-0044

ILLINOIS

Bensenville Home Society
331 South York
Bensenville, IL 60106
708-289-2395

Lutheran Child & Family Services
815 W. Sigwalt
Arlington Heights, IL 60005
708-628-6448

INDIANA

Adoption Program
Planned Parenthood of East Central Indiana
110 North Cherry Street
Muncie, IN 47305
317-286-3700

Catholic Charities
120 South Taylor
South Bend, IN 46601
219-234-3111

Sunny Ridge Family Center
9105 A Indianapolis Blvd., #301
Highland, IN 46322
219-838-6611

KENTUCKY

University of Kentucky
429 Lynnway Drive
Winchester, KY 40391
606-257-4407

LOUISIANA

Catholic Community Services
4884 Constitution Ave., #1-B
Baton Rouge, LA 70808
504-927-4930

Diocese of Baton Rouge
4884 Constitution Ave., #1-B
Baton Rouge, LA 70808
504-927-4930

Jewish Family Services
3611 Rue Colette
New Orleans, LA 70131
504-524-8475

MASSACHUSETTS

Hampshire Community Action
Skyline Trail
Chester, MA 01011
413-584-4434

Work/Family Directions
930 Commonwealth Avenue
Boston, MA 02215
617-278-4168

MICHIGAN

Adoption Consultants of Michigan
20600 Eureka, Suite 705
Taylor, MI 48180
313-282-1137

Child and Parent Services
15728 Angelique
Allen Park, MI 48101
313-381-3570

MINNESOTA

Children's Home Society of Minnesota
2507 Burnham Road
Minneapolis, MN 55416
612-646-6393

Children's Home Society of Minnesota
4423 Arden View Court
Saint Paul, MN 55112
612-646-6393

MISSOURI

Worldwide Love for Children
1601Q West Sunshine
Springfield, MO 65807
417-869-3151

NEW HAMPSHIRE

Child & Family Services of New Hampshire
99 Hanover Street
P.O. Box 448
Manchester, NH 03105
603-668-1920

NEW JERSEY

Golden Cradle
2201 Route #38
Executive Building, 8th Floor
Cherry Hill, NJ 08002

Growing Families Inc.
1 Tall Timber Drive
Morristown, NJ 07960
201-984-7875

OHIO

Gentle Care Adoption Services
243 East Livingston Avenue
Columbus, Ohio 43215
614-469-0007

OKLAHOMA

Hannah's Prayer Adoption
    Agency
2651 East 21st Street, Suite 409
Tulsa, OK 74114
918-743-5926

OREGON

Open Adoption & Family Ser-
    vices
529 Grand Avenue
Portland, OR 97214
503-233-9660

TEXAS

Adoption Advocates
800 N.W. Loop 410, Suite 355
San Antonio, TX 78216
512-344-4838

Adoption Services Association
8703 Wurzbach
San Antonio, TX 78240
512-699-6088

Catholic Counseling Services
3845 Oak Lawn Avenue
Dallas, TX 75219
800-833-5878

Home of Saint Mark
1302 Marshall
Houston, TX 77006
713-522-2800

Life Anew, Inc.
2635 Loop 286 N.E.
Paris, TX 75460
903-785-7701

Methodist Mission Home
6487 Whitby Road
San Antonio, TX 78240
512-696-7021

Valley Baptist Medical Center
3003 Granite
Mission, TX 78572-9742
512-580-3660

UTAH

Children's Service Society of
    Utah
576 E. South Temple
Salt Lake City, UT 84102
801-355-7444

CANADA

Adoption Resource & Counseling
162 Phillips Street
Kingston, Ontario K7M 228
Canada
613-542-0275

Hope Adoption Services
P.O. Box 8000-531
Abbotsford, British Columbia
V25 6HI
Canada
604-263-1372

Index

Abortion, 14, 15, 16, 18, 24, 35, 39, 68, 79, 89, 92

Adopted child(ren): and adopting parents, relationship between, 5, 47–49, 64–65, 127–151; birth of, 11, 22–23, 47–48, 86, 98, 100–105, 119, 159; and birthparents, relationship between, 5, 47–49, 70, 110–126, 132–138, 142–148; bonding with, 149–150; in closed adoptions, 28–29, 30–40, 42, 135–138; confusion about true parents, 143–148; heritage of, 129–133; joys of, 179–182; and knowing why their birthparents had them adopted, 133–134; letter to, from birthparents, 133–134; name of, 48–49; peer and so-cietal treatment of, 139–141; self-esteem of, 133; and talking about the adoption, 138–139; time between birth and finalization of adoption, 106–108

Adopting parent(s), 5, 9–11; and adopted child, relationship between, 5, 47–49, 64–65, 127–151; adopted child's confusion about, 143–148; age of, 1, 9, 37, 38, 75, 85, 95, 127, 158; at birth of child, 11, 22–23, 47–48, 86, 98, 100–105, 119, 159; and birthmother's change of mind, 11, 34–35, 85–87, 100–102, 159, 163–164; and birthparents, relationship between, 5, 12, 42, 44–49, 70, 74–76, 78–82,